WHAT AM I THAT YOU CARE FOR ME?

Carlo-Maria Martini

What am I
that you care for me?

Praying with the Psalms

ST PAULS

Original titles:
  Che cosa è l'uomo che te ne curi?
© 1988 Editrice Elle Di Ci, Leumann (Torino), Italy

  La Scuola della Parola
© 1985 Arnoldo Mondadori Editore S.p.A., Milano, Italy

Translated from the Italian by Dame Mary Groves, OSB

Cover illustration: 'Revelation 19:11-13' by Elizabeth Dangrow

ST PAULS
Middlegreen, Slough SL3 6BT, United Kingdom
Moyglare Road, Maynooth, Co. Kildare, Ireland

English translation © ST PAULS (St Paul Publications) 1990
First print 1990, reprinted 1994

ISBN 085439 347 1

Printed by The Guernsey Press Co. Ltd, Guernsey, C.I.

ST PAULS is an activity of the priests and brothers of the Society of St Paul
who proclaim the Gospel through the media of social communication

Contents

PART II

The school of the word
Reflections on Psalm 50

Foreword

For over a decade the Church in Milan has been guided and inspired by its Cardinal Archbishop, Carlo-Maria Martini, the noted biblical scholar and outstanding Pastor. Open to today's problems and concerns, the cardinal has always been in constant dialogue with his people, sharing their hopes and fears. His discussion groups and meetings, especially with young people, at the Cathedral of Milan are now a well-known regular feature.

The reflections on the psalms in this book are taken from the talks given by Cardinal Martini at these meetings. We believe that the readers will benefit from these shared thoughts which embody a profound human and religious experience in a sustained meditation on the Word of God.

The Publishers

PART I

What is man
that thou art mindful of him?
(Psalm 8:4)

*The book of Psalms is like a garden which contains the fruits of all
other books, grows a crop of song and so adds its own special fruit
to the rest. It seems to me that for a person who recites them the
psalms are like a mirror in which one may see oneself and the
movements of one's heart and mind and then give voice to them.*

St Athanasius

1
Having faith

PSALM 130 [RSV:131]

> O LORD, my heart is not lifted up, my eyes are not
>   raised too high;
> I do not occupy myself with things
>   too great and too marvellous for me.
> But I have calmed and quieted my soul,
>   like a child quieted at its mother's breast;
>   like a child that is quieted is my soul.
>
> O Israel, hope in the LORD
>   from this time forth and for evermore.

Today I have been thinking of what St Paul wrote to the
Thessalonians: "For not only has the word of the Lord
sounded forth from you in Macedonia and Achaia, but your
faith in God has gone forth everywhere, so that we need not
say anything" (1 Thess 1:8).

Everything that is good in what I have to say comes from
God working through your desire for prayer, silence and
attention to the Word. We will concentrate particularly on
the Word of God as source of prayer, and learn to read the
Word of God as food for prayer, and a guiding light for our
lives.

We want to listen to the Word of God so that it can become
prayer in us and throw light on our being. It is not easy, but
it is the aim of this exercise of prayerful listening to the
Word of God. We need the Spirit of God to enlighten us, and
I earnestly pray for that intention.

The psalms as prayer

This is an exercise to help you to understand the psalms better.

The psalms I have chosen take us on a kind of journey. They have been arranged in a particular order, following humanity's path towards God, and through them we hope to understand the way individuals and all humanity must search for God.

The first two psalms are intended to illustrate the starting point; the psalms which follow consider some of the focal points in the journey of life; and the last psalm will be the close of this journey, when a person begins to praise God fully. Praise is the goal of the human journey.

We cannot study the psalms at length. However, we may say that they are songs offered up to God by the people of God. They are prayers. Occasionally we shall have to analyse them a little but that is solely in order to facilitate our prayer. They are a means by which God teaches us to pray. And they are sung prayers, not only coming from the lips but prayers in which the whole person is involved, in feeling, thought and imagination.

So the psalms are poetry and, for this reason, full of images. They need to be sung, at least interiorly, if we wish to grasp their message.

They are prayers, then, sung prayers, belonging to the people of God. Therefore we should recite them not just as ancient prayers, but also as prayers of the people of God today. They are the prayers which God puts on his people's lips today; they teach us what the Church of today ought to ask of God, what she should hope for. So let us try to meditate on the psalms, entering into that rhythm of poetry and prayer that they, by God's inspiration, seek to impart to us.

Our journey towards God

Let us meditate on a psalm which I believe is appropriate for the start of our journey towards God. It is one of the shortest in the psalter, comprising only three verses. It might even seem too simple, for it is a psalm about which there is nothing much to say because it is already made quite plain by its own words.

Nevertheless, under its apparent simplicity this psalm conceals many problems and raises many questions. So let us try to understand it, asking the Lord to give us a truly simple heart, capable of receiving the Word of God in a manner that will allow us to fathom its depth.

Now I would like you to recollect yourself with me in prayer and ask God for the gift of looking at the psalm in a spirit of simplicity and truth:

"Lord, we thank you for putting us in the presence of your Word which you inspired in your prophet. May we approach this Word reverently, attentively, and humbly. May we not despise this Word but receive all it has to say to us. We know that our hearts are closed, often incapable of comprehending the simplicity of your Word. Send your Spirit to us so that receiving the Word in truth and simplicity, our lives may be transformed by it. Let us not be resistant, Lord; may your Word penetrate us like a two-edged sword; may our hearts be open to it; let not our eyes be closed, nor our minds wander, but may we give ourselves entirely to this listening. We ask this, Father, in union with Mary who used to recite the psalms, through Jesus Christ our Lord."

Before we go any further, let us read this psalm (130) reflectively. As you see, it is made up of three very short verses.

— In the first verse, which is a description of what we ought not to do, there is a series of negative phrases: "My heart is not lifted up, my eyes are not raised too high, I do

15

not occupy myself with things too great." So this first verse defines what a person before God does not want to be, ought not to be, and yet feels that this is how it is, and longs for it to be otherwise.

– The second verse on the other hand expresses what in reality a person is before God, and wants to be before God: "I have calmed and quieted my soul like a child quieted at its mother's breast, like a child that is quieted is my soul." This second verse invokes the image of a child in the arms of its mother.

– The third verse, however, takes this scene, which seems purely individual, and applies it unexpectedly to the whole people of God. This says that it is valuable not only for one person but for everyone.

Now problems and questions begin to arise. This psalm is not so clear and obvious as it seems.

Take for example the first verse: "I do not occupy myself with things too great." Why? Is it not a characteristic that people have, this need continually to rise above themselves, to look for something more and better, and achieve something greater? The second verse with its picture of the child in its mother's arms is still more unsettling: "But how can anyone sleep like that when the world is in agony; how can I desire that placid state as an ideal when everything around is in turmoil?" Can we accept this psalm as it stands? What is it really trying to say to us? Is all that we have to hope for a tranquil sleep?

It is not easy to understand the message. So let us read the psalm once again and grasp what it is really trying to say.

We shall begin with what seems the simplest part: the picture of the baby in its mother's arms. Even from a linguistic point of view, as a translation it is not easy to grasp because the picture which immediately comes to mind is that of a child a few months old, crying and kicking because it wants milk. Then once it has had the milk, it quietly goes to sleep in its mother's arms. This seems the right picture: a child that has been fed is quiet. In reality, however, our text speaks of a weaned child, an infant past the first stage in its life. But according to what we know of the ancient world, the Hebrew world, the world of the East, and the indications given in the Bible, the period for breast-feeding before weaning was comparatively long.

Thus the Hebrew word does not correspond to the English word. It is a noun which means: "a three-year-old child". A child who has come to the end of the breast-feeding cycle can already move about, walk and talk. And so it seems to me that the psalm intends to say something more than what we understood at first: it is a child which has already begun to recognize its mother, to identify her consciously as a person to be completely trusted. It is a child already able to move around, to play and encounter others, and at one point it has been frightened because it found itself confronted with someone or something bigger than itself. So it runs to hide in its mother's arms and there to be at peace again. It is a child who at the first instant of confrontation with life knows where it has a secure point of reference and from where it can start off again to face life afresh.

This second verse can then be read in a sense which will give full meaning to the original Hebrew text. And if we can read something more into these words than we saw at first glance we can also try something similar by re-reading the first verse.

Where the translation says: "my heart is not lifted up" the Hebrew says: "my heart does not rise up, does not go up to the heights, and my eyes are not raised up above."

What can we read into this? In reality these are expressions which go back to the cult of the high places, the cult of idols set on the mountains to which men looked for immediate aid. Here, then, it is not simply talking about a man who has come to a certain mediocrity of existence and so has learned to renounce higher desires out of a kind of philosophical asceticism, saying: "It is best not to want much in life, because there is little to be got out of it"; it is not a man who has decided with a somewhat weary maturity to balance desires against their realization, restricting the scope of his desires.

Such a type is far from the man in the psalm, who seeks

the worth and greatness of his true self, not in idols, nor in the work of his hands, nor in his dreams of power. It is a man who, having repudiated all forms of idolatry, recognizes that true greatness is found only in God.

This "not looking for things too great" – not proudly raising one's eyes – means for the man in the Bible that "God alone is great"; hence he is a man who realizes the infinite greatness of God. Before this greatness he feels himself to be poor, to be nothing, but in his nothingness he finds his true self.

There is another expression in this first verse which is worth understanding better: "I do not occupy myself with things too great". This too is a rather poor translation, because in reality the Hebrew says: "I do not walk in, that is, I do not go after, I do not express my humanity by the things that make the most noise; I do not go by appearances but base myself firmly on God's absolute truth."

You see that, gradually, in seeking to understand the psalm, we leave a somewhat too obvious, too literal interpretation, (as though it were a psalm of tranquil simplicity attained by mediocrity, the smothering of desires). Instead we enter into the heart of the meaning of the psalm: this is a man who realizes that God is all, that God alone is great, that God can be trusted unconditionally, and that therefore in God anything can be attempted because, even though what we do may appear small to ourselves, everything acquires value in the eyes of God.

So we have tried to understand a little what is behind the words of the psalm, to see the spiritual insight in which it has its roots. It is the profound sense of God as absolute, God as our strong bulwark, God as the reality in which we can blindly trust, before whom we are not non-entities, and in whom everything is possible.

There is nothing greater than the strength we have when we do everything in God, when we act in accordance with the truth daily revealed to us, when we no longer walk according to our own whims but in the truth of God.

This then is the message of the psalm. And at this point we can put some questions to ourselves which will lead us into prayer and meditation. The questions might be these: What does this psalm say to the people of God? What does this psalm say to me personally? What do I say to God in this psalm?

– *What does this psalm say to the people of God?* We have said that the last line of the psalm, which seems to be entirely personal ("O Israel, hope in the Lord, both now and for ever") shows that in reality it is a psalm for all the people. We ought then to ask ourselves what this psalm is saying to the people of God. Throughout the Old Testament this people is said to be one which has fixed its gaze on hope in the infinite God, his infinite mercy, his infinite power, his infinite greatness.

Therefore the people which knows God's greatness, and adores him in truth, is the people which is filled with hope. Certainly it will also be a people which will have its own culture, its own civilization, its own future; but it will not be a people which will treat these things as idols, trusting solely in its own works and therefore falling into one illusion after another. Instead, this people will set before itself that absolute hope in God which never fails.

What does the psalm say to the people of God *now*? What does it say to the Church today? Do we know, as a Church, how to have absolute hope in God? Do we put our faith in our own works or in God alone, from whom comes the power for the work of our hands? Are we capable of this abandonment to the Word?

– *What does this psalm say to me?* Each one of us can ask: What is my faith in God? What is my abandonment to him? Do I feel the serenity of abandonment to him or is there deep within me much anxiety, anguish and fear, because I have not yet accepted God's supremacy?

And then we can apply this psalm to ourselves in the words of the New Testament: "If you do not turn and become

19

like children you will not enter the Kingdom of heaven" (Matthew 18:2). It is necessary to attain to this absolute simplicity of abandonment to the great God.

Above all, we can make our own the words of Mary: "My soul magnifies the Lord, because he has regarded the lowliness of his handmaiden" (Luke 1:48). This is the psalm of our Lady, who did not walk in things beyond her, but found entire fulfilment in the power of God manifesting itself in her.

– *What do I say to God through this psalm?* Am I able to recite it, accepting its total rejection of empty, useless hopes, and knowing that forever my hope is solely in God, to whom I can abandon myself in complete faith?

Let us ask in prayer that this absolute certainty may become the foundation of our life, and that all our actions may be blessed by that sure hope.

2
Our response

Blessed is the man
   who walks not in the counsel of the wicked,
nor stands in the way of sinners,
   nor sits in the seat of scoffers;
but his delight is in the law of the LORD,
   and on his law he meditates day and night.
He is like a tree
   planted by streams of water,
that yields its fruit in its season,
   and its leaf does not wither.
In all that he does, he prospers.

The wicked are not so,
   but are like chaff which the wind drives away.
Therefore the wicked will not stand in
   the judgment,
nor sinners in the congregation of the righteous;
   for the LORD knows the way of the righteous,
but the way of the wicked will perish.

"Blessed is the man"

This psalm which you have just read is not a prayer. You
know that the psalms are the prayers of the People of God,
but this – the first psalm – is not a prayer; it is rather an
exclamation and a *blessing*: "Blessed is the man". To
understand it really as an exclamation, that is, as the

expression of a strong inward emotion, we have to find the root from which it springs, the intuition from which it flows. It is a blessing: "Blessed is the man who follows not the counsel of the wicked", which goes with the blessings on those who enter the Kingdom: "Blessed are you poor, blessed those who hunger and thirst for righteousness" (Matthew 5:3,6). It is to be seen along with the blessing of Mary: "Blessed are you who have believed" (Luke 1:45); or with the blessing on those who listen to the Word proclaimed by Jesus: "Blessed are those who hear the Word of God and put it into practice" (Luke 11:27).

This psalm expresses an exclamation coming from a profound understanding of the human race.

It is almost an anthropological introduction to the whole psalter: it has been put at the beginning precisely as an introduction to all the prayers of the psalter to show what humanity is, what kind of person one who prays is. So we ought to read it with this question in mind: What sort of person can be called happy, that is, fulfilled? The question of course which follows immediately is whether we can be compared to this type of person, whether our society, our way of life, can be so compared.

Now we will read the psalm again bearing these questions in mind. It is very simple, seemingly far too simple, were it not that in reality it is a synthesis of Hebrew thought, a synthesis of what Judaism maintained a person should be before God and history. We will re-read it part by part; then we will try posing some questions in order to find out what the psalm is saying.

Who is a just person?

The psalm divides easily into three parts: the first tells us about the just man. First of all, it says what the just man is not (he is one who does not do certain things, and does do others), and then it describes this just man by a comparison: the tree beside a stream.

The first part of the psalm, therefore, is a very simple portrait of the person who lives uprightly. The second is the opposite picture, a portrait of someone who is called wicked: who he is, what he is to be compared to, what his fate is. The third part is a conclusion: how God acts toward the one and the other.

Now let us read each verse separately, trying to understand what they are saying to us with their images. First of all, they describe the psalmist's idea of the just man: he is defined with three negative and two positive characteristics. The negative ones are: he does not follow the counsel of the wicked, does not linger in the way of sinners, does not sit in the company of scoffers – these are three things the just man does not do.

In some translations this does not come out clearly enough. The Hebrew text describes the three things the just man does not do by referring to three fundamental movements: walking, standing, and remaining seated or lying down. These are three positions in which a person can behave negatively. Notice how this triple negative is described, not as something the person does on his own account, but as a member of society: "Blessed is the man who walks not in the counsel of the wicked, nor stands in the way of sinners, nor sits in the company of scoffers"; that is, the man is described according to his physical make-up and also according to his association with others in a group.

This negative behaviour on the part of a person is presented as identifying with a group, a mentality, a culture, we would say today, with a negative outlook.

This is the description of someone who is *not* a just person: it is a person who lets himself or herself be drawn along by a mentality, a culture, an ambience, a world view, a philosophy, which is characterized by being negative, unjust, uncaring.

The two following lines describe, on the other hand, what the just person is. And here too it is interesting to see that the description is not what we expect at first sight. We might think that the just man is the one who does not do certain things and acts uprightly, knows what it is to be good to others, serves his neighbour, says his prayers... Here, the just man is described by means of a much more fundamental feature: he is described in relation to what he loves.

The translation says he takes pleasure in the Law of the Lord; the Hebrew text is stronger: "The law of the Lord is his joy", that is, the Law of the Lord is his love, his predilection, what he has chosen. It is his first choice, his life-long choice.

The man is being described in relation to what he loves and also, on that account, by what he thinks about, day and night. It is the language of love, of the lover, something that has sunk in and comes out again through the heart and the mind. He meditates on the Law day and night; and the word "meditate" translated also signifies a physical action, that is, muttering, murmuring with the lips.

So the idea is that of a man who savours the Law by day and by night, makes it his food. Here we see the venerable figure of a rabbi repeating by heart almost without interruption the Law of the Lord.

That is the description of the just man, according to what he does and does not do, or better, according to what he loves and has at heart, what he always has with him: the Law of the Lord, which he meditates day and night without interruption; there is not an instant when he is not in love with the Law.

Then this man is described again with a comparison: like a tree planted by running water, which gives its fruit in season. This seems a somewhat ordinary illustration; but we know that in Palestine running water is scarce and a tree planted by water is more or less a rarity, a luxury, and for this reason it is in an exceptionally favourable situation. This tree planted by a stream sinks its roots into the soil bathed by the water and therefore follows the productive rhythm of the seasons. Hence it bears fruit at the right time and its leaves never fade. Then the comparison is summed up like this: "In all that he does, he prospers." The everyday reality is that all his undertakings hit the mark, or according to a translation nearer to the Hebrew: "God makes all he does come out right." Clearly this is not in the sense of instant success, but in the sense in which we ask in the *Our Father*: "Thy Kingdom come", that Kingdom which will come, without fail. One who has set his love on the Law will not be deceived; all that he does is on the right road for building the Kingdom, and he will not have to regret being led by this inner love.

That is the first part of the psalm. The second, on the other hand, describes by contrast the wicked man, one who does not practise righteousness. "Not so, not so, but like chaff blown away by the wind": the picture is that of someone who does not succeed in building, for things slip from his hands, he cannot hang on to anything. Thus, the image could recall the dispersion of humankind when trying to build the Tower of Babel to reach the sky. They attempted to make a name for themselves by this tower but their internal confusion dispersed them, and so they do not succeed in building a city, in producing unity.

"Therefore the wicked will not stand in the judgment." This is probably an allusion to the final judgment, the judgment on history. Those who belong to the category of the wicked do not build history because the judgment on history finds them wanting.

The psalm ends with a reassuring word. "The way of the just is known to the Lord." It brings out the loving consciousness, the tender care of God for the way of the just man, whereas the way of the wicked is not actually described as being under the wrath of God, but simply as something which does not succeed, which falls to pieces and is lost.

This is the immediate reading of the psalm which, as you see, is very simple in expression and contains symbols which Christian antiquity made a point of adopting later. These flowing waters are, in the Christian tradition, the blessing of the Spirit of God, and the tree planted by the waters is the person with roots plunged into the living water of the Spirit.

One ancient Christian writer, referring to this psalm,

speaks of the wood of the Cross as the tree by which humanity bears fruit. So the symbolism of this psalm further extends to baptism: the individual immersed in the baptismal waters who bears fruit in the life of God.

The psalm, in its outward expression, is not lyrical in tone, but rather a description in the Wisdom tradition on account of the profound intuition of the psalmist.

Human existence is a choice

Let us ask ourselves, now that we have read the psalm again, what kind of discourse this is about humanity, this man-centred introduction to the whole psalter. Who exactly is the man called just here, who exactly is the man called wicked?

Notice that this anthropology is different from any purely evolutionary discourse. It is drama: it is about a man developing from good to better; it is an antithesis, a choice, a profoundly ethical and moral discussion. People are constantly faced with serious decisions which have dramatic consequences for them, for their life and for the life of the world.

Human adventure is not in fact a going from one experience to the next; but rather from one decision to the next, and each decision affects our future. This psalm is pervaded by a sense of the drama of human existence, which is a choice. A choice which can be miscalculated and definitively spoiled; a choice which is a gamble, a gamble of oneself, one's future, one's human existence. A person is made or destroyed by these decisions which are either constructive or destructive, for oneself and for others; no one escapes this dramatic reality.

This then is the meaning of the man-centred discourse of introducing the psalms, which are precisely marked by this drama of good and evil, love and hate, light and darkness, truth and falsehood — we are continually called to make choices.

After bringing out the dramatic dimension of the anthropology underlying this psalm, we can ask ourselves who the wicked, unjust man is. We could apply this first of all, on the moral level: the just man is the one who does good; the unjust man robs, kills, does acts of violence, exploits his neighbour, sows division, hatred; the just man is of service to his brother, forgives, loves, prays and adores. In this way we can analyse the twofold description at a moral level and that certainly is also within the perspective of this psalm.

We have seen however that in the description in the first lines, the point at issue is more lofty: the man is described not in relation to moral behaviour but in relation to what he loves.

Well then, who is this just man? A man who lives by the Word of God, who has chosen to love the Law, the Law taken as Torah, that is, as a proclamation of what God is for humanity and what humanity is called to be in the Word of God. In reality, then, this psalm describes the blessedness of the person who has understood that we are what we are, not simply by force of moral perfection but by having reference to the Word of God, letting ourselves be nourished by the Word, letting ourselves be plunged in the Word like the roots of the tree in the water.

The reference to human joy is this capacity to meditate on the Word, to make it our food day and night without ceasing, embracing the whole of our experience, knowing that no aspect of our experience is foreign to the Word of God and the message of his Word.

The man called happy, successful here, is the one who has understood that we cannot create ourselves, generate ourselves, and so feel just and true. We have to accept the Word of love which God gives. This Word reveals me to myself; what I am called to be; the greatness of my call; the hope to which my life is committed; the world's hope. A person who has grasped this is the just man, *one who lives a moral life*. Human morality, then, is bound up with our human capacity to be interrogated by this Word which created us and looks into our very depths.

And who is the unjust man? The unjust man is one who does not risk accepting the pre-eminence of the Word, does not risk admitting what horizons open up to us in our lives if we know how to receive the Word of God.

Obviously the Word has many ways of reaching the human heart; some of its ways are found within ourselves, calling us to truth, justice, the gift of self. Nevertheless we are always characterized by this ability we have to rise above our narrow egoism and receive the Word which invites us to give ourselves to God and the service of others. A person like this is characterized not by a morality of works but by a morality of fruits: here is the tree planted by a stream which will give its fruit in due season, not a person who performs exterior actions driven solely by inner compulsion but one who flourishes and bears fruit: that is, whose actions are the loving, reasonable, true extension of himself.

Such a person is fully authentic, and a society composed of such people is an authentic society, a society bearing fruit in the sense of being not only structured outwardly but built from within by the will and actions of its members.

Towards a fruitful morality

This is the morality of the one who listens to the Word. This morality bears fruit in due season, which is to say that a person is long in maturing, needing time for growth, in harmony with the self and the universe.

This is the picture of humanity and human morality portrayed by the psalm.

We can ask ourselves a few questions. I suggest three on which we might reflect, asking God to give us the light of his Word.

First question: Do I truly live the Word of God? That is, is the Word something which fills my heart, feeds me, or is it still something outside me, distant? If we look deeply into ourselves, we shall see that the Word is closer to us and our life than we could perhaps express at first. But let us note at once that there can be no general answer to the question "Do I live the Word?" There needs to be a definite response and that is to ask: How much time do I give to the Word in my life?

Let us remember what the psalm says: "And on his law he meditates day and night." Now if I look at the ordering of my days and nights, how much time do I give to listening to the Word? And conversely, how much time do I devote to what is blown away, "like chaff blown by the wind", to dissipation? Let us seriously ask ourselves how much time we can take, with no harm done, from what can be indiscriminate television viewing, losing time with no particular purpose, and devote it instead to listening to or reading the Word of God. Without that time, clearly we shall not live by the Word of God and so it will have no power in us. Do we live by the Word? How much time do we give to listening to the Word? What time do we want to give morning and evening, during the day and at night, blessing the rhythm of our days and nights, to listening to the Word?

Second question: What actions make us live by the Word? To live by the Word means all those actions which are the fruit, the genuine expression, of myself in regard to others. Let us ask ourselves what actions make us live by the Word, what actions are the sign in us of the working of the Word we have heard: what acts of forgiving, controlling our feelings at home, controlling our emotions, controlling our imagination, our thinking, our bodies. Controlling everything that can be instinctive reaction is a fruit of the Word. Do I express in my body that I am fed by the Word and live by it? In short: do I live by the Word? What actions make me live by the Word?

Third question: How shall I live next Christmas or Easter holidays to show that I am living by the Word? Will it be a time of dissipation, like chaff blown away by the wind? At Christmas, for example, shall we follow the general consumer fashion which carries us away each year and is difficult to avoid, or rather, shall we know this year how to make provision for a moment's sacrifice, charity, good work, community service, that will show a Christmas spent welcoming the Word made flesh?

Let us ask Mary Immaculate who received the Word in herself to give us that experience of profound inner joy welling up in this psalm. May this psalm with its simple words, seemingly not very poetic, appeal to us for what it is, a cry of the heart from one who has understood that the Word of God – God who speaks to us, reveals himself to us – is our whole life and is able to change us continuously.

3
Physical and spiritual pain

PSALM 6

O LORD, rebuke me not in thy anger,
    nor chasten me in thy wrath.
Be gracious to me, O LORD, for I am languishing;
    O LORD, heal me, for my bones are troubled.
My soul also is sorely troubled.
    But thou, O LORD – how long?

Turn, O LORD, save my life;
    deliver me for the sake of thy steadfast love.
For in death there is no remembrance of thee;
    in Sheol who can give thee praise?

I am weary with my moaning;
    every night I flood my bed with tears;
    I drench my couch with my weeping.
My eye wastes away because of grief,
    it grows weak because of all my foes.

Depart from me, all you workers of evil;
    for the LORD has heard the sound
        of my weeping.
The LORD has heard my supplication;
    the LORD accepts my prayer.
All my enemies shall be ashamed and
        sorely troubled;
    they shall turn back, and be put to shame
        in a moment.

Not an easy psalm

We now reflect on Psalm 6 which begins: "Lord, rebuke me not in thy anger, nor chasten me in thy wrath." It is not an easy psalm to understand and still less to comment on, to find the underlying meaning. Well, let us ask ourselves what these difficulties are, then we will try to make a synthesis so that we can grasp what it is saying to us, how we can live it and what conclusions to draw from it.

It is not an easy psalm for various reasons.

First it is a psalm which talks about God's anger. "Lord, rebuke me not in thy anger, nor chasten me in thy wrath." It is not easy to have an idea of this anger of God; it is something outside our ordinary vocabulary. How can we really feel drawn to pray by such an abrupt reference to the anger, the indignation of God?

There is a second reason why the psalm appears difficult to us: it seems to limit our human horizons to this world.

There is that very strange sentence towards the middle: "For in death there is no remembrance of thee; in Sheol who can give thee praise?" It looks as though anyone saying this psalm lives with no thought of a life after death but has a limited field of vision, restricting his or her horizons to this present life. The New Testament has completely transformed this view, clearly stretching our horizon to life without end.

A third reason why the psalm is not easy lies in its literary form: it is a psalm of lamentation. The definition: "lamentation psalm" evokes something not very attractive, we might almost say, painful. So why bother with a depressing psalm?

Finally, it is a psalm about illness, one of those composed to be recited over the sick and suffering.

Perhaps you have had no experience of grave illness, such as is presupposed here. How can we presume to enter into the painful state of mind of those seriously ill, tempted to despair, to close in on themselves, rejecting others? It is a painful, agonizing state of mind that only someone who has experienced it fully can describe; and certainly the one who wrote this prayer has had an experience of this kind. It is that of a sick person, anxious and alone, who feels life diminishing with no one to help him, as though everyone is against him; he is suffering from a persecution complex, and rages against society. There truly are such situations, though you have perhaps not had to live through any of them. So how can you expect to understand a situation which is no doubt true to life but outside your experience?

These are some of the main difficulties that we find when reading this psalm. Let us try to consider them together. What is the psalm saying in substance? It is a little drama with three personages: God, the sick or suffering person, the enemy. This too raises a difficulty because the reference to enemies is not very clear – who are these enemies?

A drama with three characters

So it is a man in a state of prostration who feels abandoned by God, who cries out to tell him about being abandoned, and who in calling on God feels he is heard.

This summarizes the psalm: a man in extreme physical and spiritual weakness, transfixed by the desire of his heart for God, feels angered against himself, seeks to be free of his enemies, and receives the saving word.

How does this summary match with the psalms we have already read? We have taken for consideration some psalms which tell us about seeking God, about humanity's route-map in search of God, and we have especially considered two psalms which speak of this search. One, Psalm 131 [130], springs from a great faith: "Like a weaned child in its mother's arms, so is my soul": this is humanity looking in faith to the God who calls. In the second psalm we meditated on the clear decision to be taken by a person on this journey between two ways which determine our earthly existence.

These two psalms show the positive aspect of humankind's journey. This one however shows the negative aspect: the emergence of that state of not knowing how to go on living, of not knowing how to find God.

How are we to succeed in grasping the message of this psalm? I think it needs a somewhat fuller explanation to make clear the two great themes which dominate all the psalms.

There are 150 psalms, all prayers which are very different from one another. They are divided, according to their content, into wisdom psalms, historical psalms (which tell the history of the Chosen People), and royal psalms (which speak of the Messiah). However, if we wanted to crystallize the fundamental attitudes of the man praying in the psalms, we would define them as an "attitude of lament" and an "attitude of praise".

The whole life of anyone who prays the psalms is permeated with praise and lament, two continually alternating rhythms of prayer, like the dual experience of dialogue and union with God.

We do not use this sort of language today to translate humanity's two fundamental attitudes in prayer: we use other words. We speak, for example, of making a request and returning thanks: the prayer of petition and the prayer of thanksgiving. But the psalter with its age-old experience of humanity, takes these two expressions of human prayer back to their roots – praise and lament.

Praise and lament in the Bible

Let us try to understand what the psalms teach us about humanity's primordial attitude towards God, the relationship with God, through praise and lament. What is praise and how does the Bible see it? Praise in the Bible has only one object: God. There is no noun in the accusative case in the Bible with the verb "to praise" other than God, for praise is the mode for humanity's attitude before God alone. And it is praise in the Hebrew sense of exultation, an enthusiastic leap of the heart, reverence and wonder at the works of God. That is biblical praise; it is the praise of the *Magnificat*: "My soul magnifies the Lord and my spirit rejoices in God my Saviour" (Luke 1:46-47).

In the Bible therefore, praise is an expression of life. We would say today, perhaps in a more philosophical form, that praise is an expression of wonder at being.

The prophet Isaiah says: "The living praise you, O God, as I do this day" (Isaiah 30:19); it is life which praises God. Praise is the dimension of conscious being, that is, of a human being conscious of being alive and praising the author of life. For the Bible, for the psalms, to praise is to live. And so not to praise is not to live.

Death is not praise of God, because not praising is the same as not living, not living the life which is God's gift, to be returned in praise. Death, understood in its negative sense as the Bible understands it, not in the sense in which we often take it as a passage to a higher and better life, but death as the negation of life, is no praise.

No praise, no life; this is not being, this is death. You see now how the psalm can say: "In death no one remembers you, can the dead give you praise?" because praise is life, to praise is to live, not to live is not to praise; praise and life correspond.

A human being feels alive when praising and feels life vibrant in enthusiastic, purposeful joy as in the psalms.

If this is praise, then what is lament, which is the opposite attitude? It is the cry of a human being whose life is diminishing; it is the cry of one who feels less life in the literal, qualitative sense of well-being, which has a proper aim in life, a proper capacity to love, a proper dignity. When a person finds these lessening, then there is lamentation; feeling the quality of life reduced, knowing that the gift of life (that is, of being) comes from the nearness to God, then he cries out: "Do not abandon me, I want to come back to praising you."

What a person feels in this lessening of life which we fear, is called here the anger of God, the wrath of God, the absence of God; because if God is life, not to live is to be abandoned by God. So then comes the cry: "Have pity on me, Lord, I am failing, heal me; my soul is quite cast down, come and free me; in your mercy, save me."

Lament is the opposite of praise, which is the consciousness that to live is to praise God. If a man senses that a part of his life is diminishing, in illness or loneliness or mental suffering, or abandonment, or fear for the future, he cries out to the God of life, and complains because God seems far away. Perhaps this will become clearer if we look at those who have prayed thus in the Bible. There comes to mind the figure of David. A large number of the psalms of lamentation are attributed to David, who passed through times of suffering, humiliation, abandonment: but he looked on his experiences as a believer, that is, as one crying out to God. He did not live through them in despair as though alone but his complaint is that of one who feels forsaken and yet knows his cry will be heard. David experienced these things.

The prophet Jeremiah wrote lamentations very similar to these psalms in language and mode of expression. He too, because of his prophesying, lived through that experience of being forsaken, and expressed his situation in a cry of lamentation. Job in his physical and mental suffering expressed himself in the same way. Jesus on the Cross did the same: "My God, my God, why have you forsaken me?"

Every Christian can relive the experience of David, Jeremiah, Jesus. There are so many circumstances in life where the Christian relives this reality. How many of our brothers and sisters in loneliness, suffering and downright persecution are living out the drama of the sixth psalm!

We should not think that those under persecution or suffering for the sake of the Gospel, for love of justice or liberty, live in a state of enthusiasm and euphoria. Often indeed they live under a tremendous burden of loneliness and fear, crying out to God without ceasing.

When we say this psalm we unite ourselves in prayer with those who suffer. Perhaps we cannot join in their suffering or offer them consolation but with this psalm we can join in the universal lamentation of those who call on God the Saviour.

I recall a striking illustration of this state of suffering and abandonment. A few days ago I made my New Year visit to the Pio Albergo Trivulzio, where there are many very old people (two or three die every day). I was very saddened by a little old man, of about seventy. I was told: "He is letting himself die, he no longer eats, he has fallen into a state of lethargy from which we can no longer rouse him." That is a very sad and true picture of life and hope and faith dwindling.

How can we even begin to describe such suffering if we have not experienced it ourselves? Let us try to understand the significance of lament in this psalm.

It starts off with the clear idea of God, Lord of life and of praise, who in love gives life to us. The lamentation is a human attempt, to reach the God of life that we feel is missing when we experience suffering.

We can also recognize the enemies the man in the psalm is speaking of when he stands there praying: "All my oppressors will retire in confusion, my enemies shall be ashamed and sorely troubled. Leave me, all you who do evil." They can be all sorts of enemies: political enemies such as invading nations, oppressors, all those who take away freedom; personal enemies too, powerful people, exploiters, unfair competitors, persecutors. The enemies in the psalm recur often though they are somewhat vague figures, without a definite form or face, but they are always people without God. They symbolize how impossible it is for the world to live without love and praise. They are the sign of the evil, the conflict, into which humanity falls when there is a lessening of freely-given praise. They are the sign of the want of praise and rejoicing, the want of truth, the predominance of violence and fanaticism, where praise and unselfishness are no longer cultivated. That is how people are in a world of egoism where all are enemies of one another, concerned only with self.

This then is the situation from which the psalm starts out. We can ask ourselves as we come to the end of these reflections: What has all this to say to me? What does the psalm mean by its mode of expression and the way it would have us pray?

The psalm poses some questions which I would like to put to you.

– The first question concerns the equation we have underlined between praising and living. Have I yet experienced the joy of losing myself in a freely given praise, that praise in which we gain the freedom which is God's? Praise can be understood as more than thanksgiving because thanksgiving, in a sense, is commensurate with the gift. Praise on the contrary, is a going beyond oneself: "We praise you, O God, for your great glory and power, we praise you because you are great in yourself; we praise you, Lord, because you are God." Or as the Bible says sometimes, as if giving a present to God: "To you, all-powerful Lord, be praise, glory, power and blessing."

If we lose ourselves in this prayer we find ourselves; that is, we feel born to praise, to find our true nature in this free and positive act. We realize the greatness of our being, that we are made for love and self-giving, in this simple act of giving praise.

For this reason perhaps praise does not often enter into our prayer, or at least it appears to be something added on, but if we try to make it our own we shall see what breathing-space, what inner freedom it gives us to put ourselves sincerely on the wavelength of praise.

– The second question turns on the theme of lamentation as the truth of our early life. The lamentation we have been trying to look at expresses the will to live, the hope of finding reasons for living in the God of life. Perhaps the definition "prayer of lamentation" used by the exegetes to indicate this psalm is not suited to us; we could call it a prayer of suffering; that is; the prayer of those who, consciously living their own sufferings and miseries, and the miseries and sufferings of their friends and of the world, offer them freely to God with trustful hearts.

– The third question makes us ask about the subject of

this lamentation. What is the man lamenting about? What is the subject of the prayer of suffering? It is everything which takes away life or which diminishes us. Here we also get the sense of the dignity of protest against everything we have in us and around us which has the force of death; protest at what is happening in the trouble-spots of the world, protest at what is happening in certain Latin-American countries, against excesses committed; protest against all attacks on the dignity of the individual.

Psalm 15 emphasizes the dignity of this protest, a spiritual dignity, and indicates moreover the nature of this protest. It is a protest which searches the depths of evil; it does not stop at outward causes, but detects the origin of evil in the human heart. It is a protest which is not inert, not according to whim, not content with shouting, but which acts in hope, and with the will to change oneself and the world. It is a protest which relies entirely on God, and therefore has a spiritual dignity rooted ultimately in life.

The Lord listens to my appeal

Now we can come to our final reflection here. What is the aim of this prayer of ours, steeped in the prayer of suffering in the last part of the psalm, which constitutes a complete change of scene? The psalmist has prayed by describing himself: "I am weary with my moaning, every night I flood my bed with tears; I drench my couch with my weeping. My eye wastes away with grief; it grows weak because of all my foes." He sounds done for, but unexpectedly the tone changes: "Depart from me, all you workers of evil; for the Lord has heard the sound of my weeping. The Lord has heard my supplication, the Lord accepts my prayer." The whole prayer of suffering becomes at this moment a threefold cry of exultation: I am certain that the Lord hears me, accepts me, receives me.

Steeped in the prayer of suffering, the despondent man achieves the certainty that God is with him, and this certitude changes his outlook on life. The enemies are enemies no longer: everything which seemed hostile appears different now. Nothing can lower his dignity any more because he feels himself capable of viewing reality with new eyes and able to overcome the obstacles with renewed enthusiasm.

It is the culminating point of this psalm, this prayer of suffering. The man who is suffering, now changed interiorly, faces all his ills, all his loneliness in a way that is no longer self-destructive but creative; with the capacity for a new understanding of what at first appeared to have no way out. You see then where this prayer of lamentation takes us. Born from the sense of praise it sets us in the truth of ourselves before God.

We can conclude by asking if there is something concrete we can do to express the force of this prayer. When we pray shall we speak in our own words and let the sufferings of the world speak in us?

I would also like to propose to you a specific action related to this psalm: an attentive visit, in a truly neighbourly spirit, to the sick and to lonely old people. Could you, either alone or with others, undertake neighbourly acts on behalf of those who live this psalm in their own lives? The gravely ill, the sick in hospital, those who are sick and alone, the sick without hope, old people who feel neglected and full of complaints about everything can, with your help, transform their lament into prayer and also perhaps – why not – into praise.

Many a miracle like this happens: why should it not happen through your aid and goodwill?

4

Joy: gratitude for life

PSALM 8

O LORD, our Lord,
    how majestic is thy name in all the earth!

Thou whose glory above the heaven is chanted
    by the mouth of babes and infants,
thou hast founded a bulwark because of thy foes,
    to still the enemy and the avenger.

When I look at thy heavens, the work of thy
        fingers,
    the moon and the stars which thou hast
        established;
what is man that thou art mindful of him,
    and the son of man that thou dost care for him?

Yet thou hast made him little less than God,
    and dost crown him with glory and honour.
Thou hast given him dominion over the works of
        thy hands;
    thou hast put all things under his feet,
all sheep and oxen,
    and also the beasts of the field,
the birds of the air, and the fish of the sea,
    whatever passes along the paths of the sea.

O LORD, our Lord,
    how majestic is thy name in all the earth!

David's experience

I don't know whether I shall be able to convey to you what I feel about this psalm. It is not so much a simple hymn of praise as a canticle of praise to God. It is a hymn of praise, and we have already seen how the two attitudes of lamentation and praise are a rise and fall of humanity's well-spring of prayer: praise for life, lament for the diminishing of life.

This time we have in front of us not simply an exclamation of praise for the grandeur of creation, nor is it even simply a contemplation of the greatness of humanity. Rather, this hymn finds its parallel in the *Canticle of the Sun* and the *Canticle of the Creatures* sung by St Francis. But not entirely. The *Canticle of the Sun* is a meditation by one who looks around and sees God's work in the sun and moon and stars, praises him for Brother Wind and Sister Water, Brother Fire and our Sister Mother Earth, for those who forgive, for our Sister Death.

Instead it seems to me that the nucleus of this psalm, while it is still a hymn of praise, is something else, and I want to try and express it by reliving the psalm in certain biblical characters who probably lived it at first hand.

It is a psalm which derives from meditation at night, a night in Palestine, under a sky luminous with stars. But it is not simply poetical contemplation of the night; it seems to me that it springs from amazement during a dramatic human event.

I picture myself the figure of David when still a warrior in the service of Saul, and there comes a time when he feels he is betrayed by the king, is trapped by his guards, and so he flees into the desert of Judaea. Into that desert which you may have seen, full of dark gorges, ravines, and precipices, David flees, and at that point night falls. So David stops; he feels alone; the enemy has lost track of him but still he is full of trepidation. Something irreparable has taken place. He has lost the king's trust, it seems that God has abandoned him, and he finds himself alone in the cold of the desert night.

It is at that moment that he raises his eyes and sees the sky above him, sees those marvellous stars which still amaze us when we gaze at them in the desert of Judaea, so clear and bright as to dazzle the eye. David starts to think: "How great God is, how immense! And after all what a small thing it is that has happened to me. Yes, I made out I was important, I thought I was somebody, and now all my good fortune has gone to ruin. But what am I before this immense universe, before this infinity of God, before this boundless wealth with which the hand of God has decked the vault of the sky?"

While David is thus plunged in contemplation he gradually becomes calmer, forgets his anxieties and calamities. He loses himself in gazing at the works of God and then he thinks: "But God loves me! After all, this whole universe is for me, God is mindful of me, God cannot deceive me, God comes to me!"

You see what is amazing about this psalm: a man aware of his poverty and his fragility, unexpectedly finds himself at the centre of the universe, in the loving presence of God.

The text says: "What is man that thou art mindful of him, the son of man that thou dost care for him?" The Hebrew text has a word which signifies the visit of God: "the son of man that you come to visit him". With these two expressions: "You are mindful of man; you visit him", the writer of the psalm has in mind the whole of salvation history: God mindful of his people. As our Lady says in the *Magnificat*: "He has helped his servant Israel, mindful of his mercy", and as Zechariah says in the *Benedictus*: "He has redeemed Israel, he has visited his people". So David – and anyone praying this psalm – before the immensity of the works of God, which for a moment have taken him out of himself, sees himself greatly loved. He realizes that in all this great universe he is an object of attentive love. He feels that the story of salvation is realized in him because God is mindful of his promises. God never abandons anyone, he visits each one, he fills our hearts in his own good time.

God's plan

David gradually passes from amazement to a clear understanding that really the world is his. To humankind has been given power over the works of God's hands: "Thou hast put all things under his feet, all sheep and oxen, and also the beasts of the field, the birds of the air, and the fish of the sea" (Psalm 8:8). And then this man recovers his freedom. At first he felt a fugitive, a slave of circumstance; now, looking to God and with the certainty that God loves him, he has recovered his true status as a free man. He is able to influence history, and to grow in truth and justice.

So the psalm becomes a psalm of praise to God who in this immense, immeasurable universe so loves this little man that he has given him this great responsibility.

The man therefore feels himself much loved and much trusted by God: he has put history into his hands. The exclamation which begins and ends the psalm: "O Lord, our God, how great is your name in all the earth" is not simply taking a contemplative, detached glance at creation, but is a profound experience of the man who feels himself loved and therefore finds again his rightful place in the cosmos and in history.

It seems to me that the nucleus of the psalm is this amazement expressed in the central question: "What is man that thou art mindful of him?" Amazement shapes and orders the whole psalm: it is divided into two main parts centering on this question.

The first part speaks of the universe, the work of God, arriving finally at man, a little lost being. The second part proceeds from man much loved by God and once more considers the whole universe of which humanity is the keynote.

Here we have another example of the human-centred perspective that occurs throughout the psalms and a return to those three great concepts: God is creator, humanity is supremely loved, the universe is God's work entrusted to humanity. These are simple statements but they give us a whole framework for anthropology and human behaviour. None of us is alone! Each of us is the object of God's love. We are made the centre of a reality for which we are responsible by faith and love. That is the way I read the psalm: the experience of amazement at being so loved, at the centre of this vast complex universe which could appear so hostile, on which however we are tempted to lay destructive hands. If the vision we have of the universe were the only one that the human race had, then humanity could appear to us either as crushed by things or full of heroic drives, straining to subject the universe and be in control. Such an attempt can lead to a destructive use of the universe so that in fact it turns against humanity.

The perspective of the psalm, on the contrary, points to the universe, the work of God, as entrusted to humanity not for use against ourselves or against others, but to make of it a canticle to the glory of God.

The Canticle of Creatures

Looking at it in this light, we once again consider St Francis' vision in the Canticle of the Sun, and we find that it is not the canticle of a man contemplating the universe in peaceful tranquillity but that of an exhausted, blind, dying man who yet has the strength to recognize the greatness and goodness of God.

It seems to me then that we can try to understand the dramatic power of this psalm because it does not spring from contemplation alone but also from a living experience. So, to help you meditate on this psalm, I suggest three lines of thought to follow in reading it, which you might consider in depth in a moment of silence and which ought also to bring you to some practical conclusions. The first line to follow is an anthropological reading of the psalm, that is, with humanity at the centre; the second is Christological, and the third eucharistic.

Guidelines

A person-centred reading suggests taking the psalm as a question: Who am I? What am I at this point in my life? What am I, small and poor as I am? I am called upon to admit in prayer: "Lord, I am nothing before you, but you are great and you are mindful of me!" So my poor self can express itself in praise and gratitude because God has done great things in me, so I ought to begin by acknowledging the greatness of God's gifts to me.

Woe to us if we disparage ourselves or have a poor idea of ourselves. Each of us is great, made a little less than the angels. The Hebrew text says "a little less than God". Crowned with glory and honour: that is what I am. And so is every other person. Thus this reading points to the conclusion: honour all people. Do I really honour everyone? Do I truly honour old age? Is there in my behaviour towards an old person a sense of pity. Do I say that they are people who don't understand, or that I'm not interested in what they think? Do I keep the commandment: "Honour your father and mother"?

Do I honour those whom God has made my neighbours? Or do I turn the soul, the life, the body of my neighbour into objects of my desire, greed, covetousness, egoism, sensuality?

Not to respect a person honoured by God is to assume a possessive attitude, snatching something for oneself. This is the person-centred reading: Do I honour what God has given me, and do I honour the person next to me?

The Christological reading of this psalm, on the other hand, is suggested by certain passages in the New Testament. I am thinking in particular of the first chapter of the Letter to the Hebrews where we find the reference: "I have made him a little less than the angels, crowned him with glory and honour," referring to Christ. Or again, chapter 15 of the First Letter to the Corinthians: "I have placed all things under his feet."

A Christological reading implies that in Christ the frail

46

figure of every human being is given glory and honour by God and made Lord of life and history. Such a reading invites us to honour Christ, the Lord of life and history, the Son of God, who as man has been given all power over my life and my future.

The question which arises from this reading is: Do I acknowledge Christ, Lord of life and history? How do I think of Christ the Lord of my life? Above all, do I accept my vocation from Christ, recognizing Christ as the one who calls me to live my life according to his design? And then the prayer from this Christological reading is: "Lord, what do you want of me? Lord of my life, what do you want me to do with my life, with my future? The Father has put the whole world in your command at your resurrection. I honour you, Lord of the world and of history, and by my life I desire to acknowledge your lordship over history. I wish to make my life conform to my vocation; and in my life and work I want to assert that you are Lord over everything."

There is also a eucharistic reading: who is this God who visits each one of us, poor as we are, who cares for us, is mindful of us? It is the eucharistic Christ, centre of the life of the Church. As we say: "Lord, I am not worthy to receive you," we can say: "Lord, what am I that you care for me, what am I that you should keep me company in our church? How can I repay your care for me?"

In this eucharistic reading we find Jesus the risen Lord of the world and the Church, in the Eucharist, centre, source and fountain of the life of the Church. All things are put under his dominion; everything comes from him into the life of the community.

The Good News

I would like to end with a quotation from the first encyclical of Pope John Paul II. It seems to me a very good commentary on what I have called the nucleus of this psalm, that is, the fundamental amazement at God – the great creator of the universe, whose name none can pronounce – for what he does for all people. The Pope says: "... How precious must man be in the eye of the Creator, if he 'gained so great a Redeemer' (*Exsultet* at the Easter Vigil), and if God gave his only Son in order that man 'should not perish but have eternal life' (cf. John 3:16)." And he goes on: "In reality, the name for that deep amazement at man's worth and dignity is the Gospel, that is to say, the Good News. It is also called Christianity."

Thus this psalm could be read as a psalm of the Good News, of amazement at God's great love for humanity. "This amazement" – continues the Pope – " determines the Church's mission in the world and, perhaps even more so, in the modern world. This amazement, which is also a conviction and a certitude – at its deepest root it is the certainty of faith, but in a hidden and mysterious way it vivifies every aspect of authentic humanism – is closely connected with Christ... The Church, unceasingly contemplating the whole of Christ's mystery [and this psalm can be seen as the psalm of the whole Church amazed at the mystery of God's love for mankind in Christ] knows with all the certainty of faith that the redemption through the Cross has definitely restored his dignity to man and rendered meaning to his life in the world. And for that reason the Church's fundamental function in every age and particularly in ours is to direct man's gaze, to point the awareness and experience of the whole of humanity towards the mystery of God, to help all men to be familiar with the profundity of the Redemption taking place in Christ Jesus" (*Redemptor Hominis* 10).

Therefore we can pray this psalm together with the whole Church, and indeed with all humanity. And our amazement becomes the amazement of all who realize that they are not lost and alone in a blind and chaotic cosmos, but who know that they are dearly loved and that they are entrusted with a great responsibility for the world.

5
Crisis of faith

PSALM 72 [RSV:73]

Truly God is good to the upright,
to those who are pure in heart.
But as for me, my feet had almost stumbled,
my steps had well nigh slipped.
For I was envious of the arrogant,
when I saw the prosperity of the wicked.

For they have no pangs;
their bodies are sound and sleek.
They are not in trouble as other men are;
they are not stricken like other men.
Therefore pride is their necklace;
violence covers them as a garment.
Their eyes swell out with fatness,
their hearts overflow with follies.
They scoff and speak with malice;
loftily they threaten oppression.
They set their mouths against the heavens,
and their tongue struts through the earth.

Therefore the people turn and praise them;
and find no fault in them.
And they say, "How can God know?
Is there knowledge in the Most High?"
Behold, these are the wicked;
always at ease, they increase in riches.
All in vain have I kept my heart clean
and washed my hands in innocence.

49

For all the day long I have been stricken,
    and chastened every morning.

If I had said, "I will speak thus,"
I would have been untrue to the generation of thy
       children.
But when I thought how to understand this,
    it seemed to me a wearisome task,
until I went into the sanctuary of God;
    then I perceived their end.
Truly thou dost set them in slippery places;
    thou dost make them fall to ruin.
How they are destroyed in a moment,
    swept away utterly by terrors!
They are like a dream when one awakes,
    on awaking you despise their phantoms.

When my soul was embittered,
    when I was pricked in heart,
I was stupid and ignorant,
    I was like a beast toward thee.
Nevertheless I am continually with thee;
    thou dost hold my right hand.
Thou dost guide me with thy counsel,
    and afterward thou wilt receive me to glory.
Whom have I in heaven but thee?
    And there is nothing upon earth that I desire
       besides thee.
My flesh and my heart may fail,
    but God is the strength of my heart and my
       portion for ever.

For lo, those who are far from thee shall perish;
    thou dost put an end to those
       who are false to thee.
But for me it is good to be near God;
    I have made the LORD GOD my refuge,
that I may tell of all thy works.

A psalm born of suffering

The Lord calls us to meditate on his Word and I want to begin by reminding you of the blessing of listening to it: "Blessed are those who listen to the Word of God and put it into practice" (Luke 11:28). This is a saving word and a promise for us all.

The Lord has called us to meditate on a psalm which expresses a particular moment in the life of a Christian. The psalms we have already meditated on are psalms about discovering God and praise and the experience of suffering. This psalm tells us of a time of human temptation, personal, social, historical. It is the temptation we feel at the apparent absence of God in history. It represents therefore a particular experience, not the whole of human experience.

Often we experience, thank God, the fullness of his presence, but there are also times which come to individuals and communities, when we experience the absence, the apparent absence, of God: "My God, I cry to you and you give no reply, I call to you night and day and do not hear your voice." The present psalm is born of an experience such as this; while having a meditative character or tone, it is a psalm born of a deep suffering, a pain which at a given moment is expressed, as though it bursts out; and then, as we shall see, it is the outburst of pain that is transmuted into the contemplation of the mystery of God.

Experiencing total abandonment

Total abandonment is a very strong religious experience. This psalm is born of a believing heart. The one speaking in the psalm is certainly a believer, someone who has relied on God, and entrusted his whole life to God. And this believer at one point feels struck down, betrayed. Why?

Why do other people (individuals, groups, races, nations) who do not believe seem to prevail? The powerful who act and work unscrupulously seem to crush the believer who

51

has trusted in God. When this becomes a telling experience, either personally or collectively, then the believer is embittered and frustrated by the comparisons he makes between the self-confidence of those who have not trusted in God and his own trust in God which seems a delusion.

It is a bitter, painful experience to which God subjects those he loves.

Here we have already an important lesson to draw: we should not be surprised if we too undergo such an experience, because it is the experience of the people of God, the experience of the believer who composed this psalm. Behind it we glimpse other great believers of the Old Testament who went through the same experience. The prophet Jeremiah said: "Lord, you are for me a dried-up brook: when I looked for the water I needed the stream ran dry, you did not come to me at the right time. You have not listened to my words" (Jeremiah 15:19). Job goes further to the extent of cursing the day he was born, because God has shut him in a trap from which he can see no way out (see Job 3).

This abandonment by God is a religious experience at the extreme periphery of faith that it can sometimes lead to our loss of faith in God.

Total risk

It is interesting to see how Scripture is not afraid of these experiences; on the contrary it introduces them, because they are the experiences of those who have risked all and walk in the friendship of God.

Clearly one who does not venture much will not have these experiences. Often the saints live such experiences to the full because they have truly risked all.

If we read some of the words of St Thérèse of the Child Jesus in the last months of her life when she was racked by illness, we see her using words very similar to those of this psalm: "My God, my God, why have you forsaken me?"

This dramatic experience is the experience of the Son of

God, the experience of one who, risking everything, loves to the very end.

This psalm is born of a very great love, and so it is proper for it to express personal pain quite freely. It seems strange to us that a person thus lamenting cannot keep his mouth shut; rather, the lament is pursued in bitterness. This man compares his life with that of others and says: "My feet had almost stumbled, my steps had well nigh slipped," that is, I have been just a hair's breadth from despair.

St Paul too has expressions like this in the Second Letter to the Corinthians. At the beginning he says: "I despaired of life itself." This comparison which the believer makes between himself and those who, though not having faith, "have it good", is carried further with a very telling description. These men, these world powers, have everything. They almost think they are exempt from pain and fear, and are full of arrogance and violence. It seems like a description of certain political figures who indulge in violence with seemingly complete impunity. "They scoff and speak with malice; loftily they threaten oppression." At one point there even appears an expression of downright atheism: "How can God know? Does the Almighty take any notice?" God does not seem to care.

The bitterness evaporates

The temptation to despair is here expressed in all its frightening and unbearable harshness.

The one praying, having looked around, reflects on himself given over to bitterness the whole day: "For all the day long I have been stricken." When the day begins he looks outside and says: "Another day with no sun."

So he is forced to conclude like Job after his deliberation which runs through the whole book: "I don't understand. I have tried to comprehend, but it was hard for me to see until I went into the sanctuary of God."

This suffering has embittered the heart of a person who,

in spite of everything, has remained faithful to God: "I cannot leave the number of your sons; I understand nothing, I see nothing, but I cling to you!"

It is the experience of darkness and desolation in which nothing is clear. But he says: "Lord, I don't understand at all but I cling to you, you will not forsake me." And this experience is rewarded: "I went into the sanctuary of God."

What happened then to this man pondering over such thoughts? At a certain point he took a decision; or better, he was given the gift of not looking into himself as though he alone were the judge of everything but of putting himself on God's side. He entered the sanctuary of God, seeing things as God sees them, letting himself be carried away from his own limited view of things to God's own eyeview of the world.

It is the turning point, when bitterness might change to peaceful acceptance of a situation now seen in a completely different light.

Discovering God as friend

The change happened in two stages which are shown in the second part of the psalm.

First of all he goes through a stage of self-evaluation, we might say, a moment of truth. This man, placing himself on God's side, and looking at history in the perspective of God's judgement – which alone is the true judgement on things – understands that what we see or experience only appears to be solid. It is instead presumptuous, capable of being violent and taking the law into its own hands, and has no permanence. It brings to mind the reply Pope John Paul II gave to journalists, who were asking him about the situation in his native land: "The shrine of Our Lady of Czestochowa has been there for 400 years and still endures; other things do not endure."

You see, to put ourselves on God's side is to see things as God sees them, therefore cultivating a sense of time and reality as God knows them in the fullness of his mystery. "They are like a dream when one awakes. On awaking you despise their phantoms. Truly, thou dost set them in slippery places; thou dost make them fall to ruin. How they are destroyed in a moment." This is the wisdom of life which the man acquires when he puts himself on God's side, but it is something more because it could be wisdom bestowing a certain sense of balance, a certain interior calm.

Prayer brings us much more than that. By declaring themselves on God's side, the faithful discover that there is a treasure better than any other: the company and friendship of God.

The psalm then describes in a more tender manner the man's personal friendship with God, something which he has not been capable of knowing by himself and which is revealed to him here: "I am always with you." It is what the father told the elder son in the parable of the Prodigal Son (Luke 15:11-32): "But you are always with me; if you knew what that meant, all the rest would be but little."

After the revelation: "But I am always with you", there is a splendid description of friendship with God at a time when he had not yet manifested himself in Christ.

This inspired man has a personal friend in God: "Thou dost hold my right hand, thou dost guide me with thy counsel, and afterward thou wilt receive me into glory." There are three points at which friendship with God is seen to dispel every difficulty. The end to suffering does not come from reasoning but from the feeling of being loved profoundly and supremely.

This is the wonder of which Pope John Paul II speaks in *Redemptor Hominis*: "The wonder of the man who finds himself supremely loved by God, and when he has undergone this interiorly then his whole vision of the world is reordered in a different way, in a positive light."

"You have taken me by the hand, you will guide me, receive me," that is, my present and my future are in your hands. And then the loving exclamation: "Who else have I in heaven but you? Apart from you I want nothing on earth."

These are most loving words. We can compare them with the words Peter spoke when asked by Jesus: "Will you too go away?" "Lord, where shall we go? You alone have the words of eternal life" (John 6:67ff). And already, centuries before, this unknown believer was saying: "Whom have I in heaven but thee? And there is nothing upon earth besides thee." "My flesh and my heart may fail," that is, I may be near to death, "but God is the strength of my heart and my portion for ever." It is like hearing the saints speaking, St Francis of Assisi repeating in ecstasy: "My Lord and my God." "God is the strength of my heart and my portion for ever. For me it is good to be near God, I have made the Lord God my refuge."

Everything has fulfilment in Christ

The psalm ends, then, in contemplation, plunged in the goodness and mercy of God. It is the experience by which alone we acquire the awareness of a faith able to bring unity to life.

The Holy Father, in an audience with the Bishops of Lombardy on 15th April 1986, affirmed that a bishop has only one duty: to witness to that faith through which humanity finds the meaning of all existence. The significance of this may be difficult to grasp.

At the beginning of the psalm we see the man trying to understand, and everything seems dark and unjust. In addition he senses the absence of God. When this man enters the mystery of God's mercy which includes the whole of salvation history, the definitive word of Scripture, and the synthesis of the eucharistic mystery – when he has entered into the heart of the Eucharist his vision is rectified, and all other things take on a luminous significance.

No longer is anything without meaning. Everything has direction and purpose for one who has taken up the right position for observation in the heart of God, the heart of Christ. From that stand-point reality is seen in its true light.

We know that if through the Eucharist we have found the centre of all community experience and all history, then we shall want for nothing.

This psalm ends in the perspective of the New Testament and the death and resurrection of Jesus Christ into which we enter. In Christ, we are shown the mystery of God. In the mystery of God, everything in our lives, whether successful or not, has significance.

How to pray this psalm

We can pray this psalm by living some of the experiences the psalmist talks about. First of all the personal experiences. We can ask ourselves: in the trials of life do I feel profoundly that Christ is with me, that he does not forsake me? Am I disposed at this moment to accept that Christ is always with me and that nothing can separate me from him, neither death, nor life, as St Paul says: "No power, no might can separate me from the love of God which is in Christ Jesus our Lord" (Romans 8:38).

Then we can pray the psalm putting ourselves in the situation of the suffering Church, the persecuted Church, which finds its strength in God.

We can pray this psalm with the people of the world, expressing humanity's longing for God.

Finally, let us ask ourselves: in what way do I express this desire for God? Are my actions, my words the same as the psalm's? "If I had said, 'I will speak thus,' I would have been untrue to the generation of thy children."

Do my actions and my words express faith in myself alone, *my* power, the strength of *my* right hand, *my* might, *my* forcefulness, or do they express the certainty that God is with me, that God is with his Church, that God is with all who trust him?

Let us pray that we may know God's mercy, source of joy for us and for the world.

6
The discovery of nature:
mystery and dynamics

PSALM 28 [RSV:29]

Ascribe to the LORD, O heavenly beings,
  ascribe to the LORD glory and strength.
Ascribe to the LORD the glory of his name;
  worship the LORD in holy array.

The voice of the LORD is upon the waters;
  the God of glory thunders,
  the LORD, upon many waters.
The voice of the LORD is powerful,
  the voice of the LORD is full of majesty.

The voice of the LORD breaks the cedars,
  the LORD breaks the cedars of Lebanon.
He makes Lebanon to skip like a calf,
  and Sirion like a young wild ox.

The voice of the LORD flashes forth flames of fire.
The voice of the LORD shakes the wilderness,
  the LORD shakes the wilderness of Kadesh.

The voice of the LORD makes the oaks to whirl,
  and strips the forests bare;
  and in his temple all cry, "Glory!"

The LORD sits enthroned over the flood;
  the LORD sits enthroned as king for ever.
May the LORD give strength to his people!
  May the LORD bless his people with peace!

Perhaps you have not reflected on this psalm. It is not among those often used in the liturgy, though it is one of the psalms most studied because of its particular characteristics.

In the first place, it is probably the oldest psalm. We have here perhaps a pagan hymn of the Canaanite peoples who inhabited Palestine before the Hebrews, a hymn with parallels to be found in ancient Ugaritic and Babylonian texts. It was sung in praise of the divinity. In the sound of the storm, especially on the high mountains as in Lebanon these men felt something which made them tremble, which brought them an experience of the beyond, and they expressed these feelings in the poetic form of their pagan culture.

Psalm 28 is then an important example of how the People of God appreciated poems and sacred songs even of other cultures who approached God without knowing his real name, limiting him within the confines of their own human concepts.

It is remarkable also by its structure. It could be called "the seven-thunder psalm" because seven times thunder is mentioned. But it could also be called "the seven-voiced psalm" because the Hebrew word translated in our version as "thunder" in fact also means "voice". So it is the psalm of the voice of God. Using the symbol of thunder and what that aroused in ancient man, it celebrates the power of God's voice in history.

In addition, it is a remarkably interesting psalm because, starting out from the Canaanite original, it has been reworked and enriched in the framework of the whole of salvation history and carries with it the age-old prayer of a people.

The name of God has been introduced into the Hebrew version in all its fullness: the psalm mentions the name Yahweh eighteen times. So it is filled with the name of God; it makes life resound with the name of God, Yahweh, who is present and who saves.

Vox temporis, vox Dei

One of the most courageous opponents of Nazism, Cardinal Faulhaber, Archbishop of Monaco, took his episcopal motto from this psalm.

I visited him in 1950 towards the end of his life and I remember that he showed me a stone he had kept. It was one of the stones thrown at the windows of the Bishop's Palace in the riot when people were incited against the bishop because he opposed the Nazi regime.

His episcopal motto was: "*Vox temporis, vox Dei*", "The voice of the times is the voice of God." That can help you to understand the central theme of this psalm.

What is meant by "the voice of the times"?

The psalm speaks first of times of atmospheric disturbance when nature is let loose. Behind this image lies the whole force of nature, such as human beings experience at certain special times. For us there are few of these, though there are moments of contemplation in the silence of the mountains, or times when a sunset at sea calls us to profound reality. There is then in the psalm the voice of nature, that voice which we begin to recognize when we withdraw from turmoil.

But this voice of nature from man's primitive times came to be read in the experience of the people of God as the voice of history, the voice of historical time in which humanity fulfils its existence. Then the psalm can be read as containing allusions to the great turning-points for Israel, the great events of the Exodus, the times when the voice of God is heard in the liberation of his people: on the mountain, on the plain and in the desert.

Again, the psalm can be read with a Christian significance, in the context of those Gospel happenings when the voice of God or the voice of Christ marked out human life as a call to salvation. We think of the voice from heaven during the baptism of Jesus: "This is my beloved Son"; the voice of Jesus commanding the winds on the sea of Tiberias; the strong cry before Jesus' death, that great voice which in its power and strength changed the direction of history; we think also of the sound of a great wind which accompanied the descent of the Holy Spirit as described in the Acts of the Apostles.

Finally, the psalm suggests for each of us the world of today and its history. It reflects our lives, set in motion, upset at times and brought back to full realization at God's call. It can be read as praise of the voice of God which shatters all resistance in my life, strikes down everything that would depress me or enslave me, and opens the door to authenticity and freedom.

This is the mighty voice of God still resounding among us, proclaimed in the Church, alive in the power of the Spirit which animates us and all authentic experiences of giving, self-sacrifice, or renunciation.

This is the voice which we are invited to recognize as "the voice of the Lord of glory on the immensity of waters", "who shatters the cedars", and makes the wilderness shake." It is the voice of the faith which can move mountains. It is the voice of God which, made present to our life, becomes ours, and which is able to speak out with courage against every contrary voice.

So, the psalm proclaims the power of the voice of God whose word has created all things, in nature, in the history of peoples, in the life of Christ and in the lives of each one of us, and invites us to see the world and human existence as supported and animated by that Word.

The promise of peace

The psalm is introduced by an invitatory: "Ascribe to the Lord, O heavenly beings, ascribe to the Lord glory and strength. Ascribe to the Lord the glory of his name." We are invited to recognize that the strong and decisive reality is the initiative of God's love. We are invited to bow down before the strength of the living risen Christ bringing life to the world, to discover, weak and timid as we are, the power of God in our life.

After this introduction and the proclamation of God's power ("the voice of the times is the voice of God"), that power is bestowed on the listening people, and the psalm ends with a promise: "May the Lord give strength to his people! May the Lord bless his people with peace!"

From the recognition of the powerful voice of God in history and in my life comes the promise of strength and peace. To be able to recognize the Word of God in all the circumstances of life, as a stimulus or call, this is our peace.

How to make the Word our own

We will end our reflection with two questions which invite us to make the Word our own, seeking – as the Fathers of the Greek Church teach – to transfer it "from the head to the heart", to make it live within us because then it becomes a word of praise and a word of courage based on our own experience.

– First question: Do I recognize the primacy of the Word in my life? Do I accept my life with the certainty that it is made significant by a call, a mission?

The voice of the times is the voice of God. The voice which comes to me from the experience I am going through, read in the light of the Word, shows itself as a call, and therefore I should welcome it, giving thanks and praise.

If I do not succeed in doing this, I will ask myself why. Perhaps I do not recognize the primacy of God and his Word in my life, or accept the significance of what happens to me as it occurs? I would like this Word, revealed to me in history, to be different. How then can I understand the saving implication of what I am going through and recognize the call from God to be someone who serves, who loves, and who praises?

– The second question comes to us from the conclusion of the psalm: "May the Lord give strength to his people; may the Lord bless his people with peace!"

Peace is a gift which the Lord grants us when we are open to the power of his Word. How do we receive this gift of peace? What do I do for peace? What is actually *done* in my community, or nation, to create the atmosphere of reconciliation in our daily relationships? For so many people the "storm on the sea" can mean enemy attack and imminent death. Are we distressed at the thought that this can happen even today? What are you asking from me, Lord, what action, what word, what initiative for peace around me?

7
Everlasting praise

PSALM 150

> Praise the LORD !
> Praise God in his sanctuary;
>> praise him in his mighty firmament!
> Praise him for his mighty deeds;
>> praise him according to his exceeding greatness!
>
> Praise him with trumpet sound;
>> praise him with lute and harp!
> Praise him with timbrel and dance;
>> praise him with strings and pipe!
> Praise him with sounding cymbals;
>> praise him with loud clashing cymbals!
> Let everything that breathes praise the LORD !
> Praise the LORD !

A shout of praise

The psalter comprises 150 religious hymns, which fall into five large groups ranging in length from some fifteen psalms to forty or forty-five psalms.

We have read together Psalms 1, 6, 8 and 28 from the first group.

What particularly interests me is to find that each of the five groups which make up the psalter ends with an exclamation of praise. For example, at the end of the first book, Psalm 40 [41] finishes like this: "Blessed be the Lord, the God of Israel, from everlasting to everlasting! Amen and Amen." To conclude Psalm 71 [72], at the end of the second book, are these words: "Blessed be the Lord, the God of Israel, who alone does wondrous things. Blessed be his glorious name for ever; may his glory fill the whole earth! Amen and Amen!"

The final grouping also, which comprises the last thirty or forty psalms or so, ends with doxologies, one of which turns into a whole psalm – Psalm 150. It is as though the person who put together the psalms from various sources had wanted to set the final seal to the collection with a short composition to proclaim the fundamental attitudes underlying the whole psalter.

As we have already said at various points, praise is one of the basic components of all Hebrew prayer, together with lamentation. Of the 150 psalms, over half are psalms of praise, or of thanksgiving, and the others are lamentations and supplications. Between the two basic attitudes of praise-lament, thanksgiving-supplication, runs the prayer of humanity. They are like the two halves of human existence, like night and day, darkness and light, and they are the substance of biblical prayer.

The attitude of praise springs from the depths of the human heart. It is a way of seeing humanity as having the capacity for amazement and wonder before God. It shows that we are able to receive life as a gift, to exult before the mystery of being which is God himself. So let us now read the final psalm.

Alleluia

It is extremely simple, composed of eleven acclamations. The first ten acclamations all begin with the word "praise", which gives the composition its movement. If we remember that "praise" in Hebrew is "*hallel*" and that the abbreviated form of the name Yahweh is Yay (Ja), we see that the psalm is marked by this recurrent "*hallelu-ja*". We have then ten imperatives – "praise" – plus a subjunctive which is an indirect invitation "let everything that breathes praise" which repeats the command, making it universal.

The imperative of praise is followed, at the beginning and at the end, by an object. Who is being praised? At the beginning of the psalm the verb "praise" is followed by the name of God in Hebrew "*El*". This is the abbreviated form of *Elohim*, the primitive, cosmic name with which the Hebrews referred to God as the highest, the inaccessible, the one who is beyond all that we can think of or imagine.

The last praise has for its object the name Yahweh. (Unfortunately the translation does not show this distinction. It would need to be translated at the beginning: "Praise God in his sanctuary," and at the end: "Let everything that lives give praise to Yahweh".) Yahweh is God's "historical" name. It means the God who is with humankind, who stands by in times of trial, who crossed the Red Sea with Israel.

So the object of praise at the beginning is God as creator of nature, Lord of the universe, and at the end it is God as Lord of history. In the imperatives of the rest of the psalm, however, the ineffable name of God is no longer used, but substituted by a pronoun: "Praise *him* in his mighty firmament; praise *him* for his mighty deeds..."

After the imperative and the indication of the object, follow some qualifying phrases which we will look at: the place of praise, the motive for praise, the instruments of praise.

The place of praise is expressed in a parallelism: "Praise God in his sanctuary; praise him in his mighty firmament." We shall see what is meant precisely by these two expressions. There follows, still as a parallelism, the *motive for praise*: "Praise him for his mighty deeds; praise him according to his exceeding greatness." Lastly the *instruments of praise* are indicated: trumpet sounds, lute and harp, timbrel and dance, strings and pipes, sounding cymbals and clashing cymbals.

The place of praise

To whom is the psalm addressed and to whom is the command to praise given? If we consider the place of praise we can discover this. "Praise God in his sanctuary." Those to whom this command is directed, then, are those who stand in the sanctuary: the priests, the levites and all the people praying there, the people of God at the time of sacrifice.

For this reason we can imagine that the psalm is now addressed to us. We are the people of God, gathered round the altar, and we are invited to this praise of God.

But the second indication of place takes us to other recipients of the command: "Praise him in his mighty firmament." What is this "mighty firmament"? It is heaven, thought of as the throne of God, his celestial temple. So, the recipients of this command are not only human beings, but all God's subjects who are with God. We are all being invited to praise God, men and women on earth, and the angels of God, the heavenly company in the presence of God in the fullness of his glory.

At the birth of Jesus the angels sang: "Glory to God in the highest and peace to his people on earth," and just as we say in the *Our Father*: "Thy will be done, on earth as it is in heaven," so here the praise becomes cosmic. It is terrestrial praise responding to the celestial. This same cosmic understanding we find also in a prayer of the Roman Canon (Eucharistic Prayer I) when we ask that the sacrifice may be taken up to the heavenly sanctuary, God's altar in heaven.

The psalm means to say that the praise we give resounds through the universe, resounds to the altar in heaven, resounds where all things are perfect and complete. Our praise seems ephemeral, fleeting, but in reality it is known in the fullness of God.

Lastly, the recipients of this command are, along with the people in the sanctuary and the angels in heaven, all living things (in Hebrew: "everything that breathes", "all that has breath"). From wherever there is the breath of life, throughout the visible cosmos, there must rise, as though a part of breathing, the praise of the Lord.

Motives for praise

We praise him for his wonderful works and for his surpassing greatness, or as the Hebrew says more clearly: "Praise him for his mighty deeds."

What are God's mighty deeds? For the Hebrew reading the psalm they are evidently: the Exodus, the crossing of the Red Sea, the entry into the Promised Land, the forming of the people, the Law given on Sinai. These are all extraordinary works of God in favour of real, historical persons: Israel and every individual. They are those prodigious events which are recounted more fully in many other psalms of praise.

Psalm 106, for example, says: 'Who can utter the mighty doings of the Lord... he rebuked the Red Sea... he gave them what they asked..." And Psalm 136: "O give thanks to the Lord, for he is good, for his steadfast love endures for ever; to him who by understanding made the heavens... to him who led his people through the wilderness." These show examples of the mighty deeds of God which are briefly recalled in the final psalm.

So it can be said that Psalm 150 with its very simple words is a synthesis of all the psalms of praise. All the manifest historical reasons that Israel had for wanting to sing to their God are summed up by that simple closing phrase: "Praise him for his mighty deeds; praise him according to his exceeding greatness." It is also a summary of the psalter in the sense that from contemplation of the mighty works, people move on to contemplation of the great God. Consider for example Psalm 104: "O Lord, my God, thou art very great! ... O Lord, how manifold are thy works! ... Yonder is the sea, great and wide ... There go the ships..." God is great because his works are great.

This is also the theme taken up by Mary in the *Magnificat*:

"My soul recognizes the Lord as great (magnifies the Lord), and my spirit rejoices in God my saviour, because he has regarded the low estate of his handmaiden" (Luke 1:46-8).

Instruments of praise

There follows the enumeration of the "instruments", the orchestra of the praise of God: trumpets, harps, lutes, timbrels, strings, flutes, sounding cymbals, clashing cymbals. It is a list which includes those few instruments that Israel had for producing music. But there is also a certain order observable here. The trumpet, probably the horn, the kind sounded for example around the walls of Jericho, is the typical instrument of the priesthood; the harp and the lute are levitical instruments, while timbrels, strings, flutes and cymbals are used by the whole people as they sang and danced before Yahweh in the great temple processions.

The instruments indicate also those people who are praising God in the Temple: priests, levites and the whole people. Everyone is doing something. It is not a form of praise in which one person sings and the rest listen but in which all participate. By the enumeration of the instruments – wind, strings, percussion – are indicated all the possible human modes of bodily expression to praise God the most high.

To go a little deeper, let us consider what lies behind the words: "clashing cymbals" or "sounding cymbals" as the Hebrew says. This "sounding" is a technical word meaning the war-cry before the assault. The word, then, goes on to express the exaltedness of God, king, saviour, messiah. It is the word shouted out in procession on a festal day like a "hurrah". It is like those exclamations which are made to emphasize a significant point in a meeting (Bravo! Hear! Hear!)

In this light we can also understand two references in the Gospel of St John: "On the last day, the great day of the feast, Jesus stood up and proclaimed..." (John 7:37). This "proclaiming" from Jesus is not a strange way of behaving, but it was the way in which enthusiasm used to be expressed at the high point of praise. Jesus too gave his "shout", but it is a shout of instruction and prophetic proclamation: "Let anyone who thirsts come to me and drink" (ibid).

And John records how before the Passion, at the time of the great Passover feast, "Jesus cried out and said: "He who believes in me, believes not in me, but in him who sent me'" (John 12:44). Jesus takes up the mood of the festal season to convey his message. He enters into the praise of the people and with it expresses his proclamation.

To conclude this short analysis, we can say that Psalm 150, by its words, its structure and the images it evokes, brings the psalter to an end with a cultic expression of cosmic praise. It ends by underlining the fundamental human attitude towards God: praise.

Christian praise

Proceeding from this psalm, we can ask ourselves: What is our Christian form of praise?

The place for Christian praise is no longer the temple at Jerusalem, but Christ, temple of the Father. We praise in Christ. Christ is our mystical, but real, place for praising: "Through him, with him, in him... all glory and honour is yours, almighty Father." In Christ we find the place of perfect praise. And we, who are in Christ, the Church, his mystical Body, the visible reality of the historical Christ, we are the place of perfect praise, and through him, with him and in him we give perfect honour to the Father.

Starting from this place of praise which is the Church, the Body of Christ, the world of our time also becomes a place of praise; not a primary place, but a place that reflects the praise that we give.

For how many centuries God has been praised in our churches! Our praise joins the centuries-old praise of those who have preceded us. We are connected with this current

71

of praise, the perfect attitude, which in Christ and in our Church, in these materialistic times, is directed to the Most High God.

The place of praise for a Christian is also the world, not simply in its physical reality, but as renewed by Christ and, we might add, in so far as it is renewed and indwelt by the Eucharist. Beginning with Christ and the Eucharist, the whole universe, redeemed by Christ, becomes a place of perfect praise.

Christian reasons for praise: the most perfect Christian transcription of the words of the psalm: "Praise him for his mighty deeds; praise him according to his exceeding greatness," is the introduction to the Eucharistic Preface: "Father, all-powerful and ever-living God, we do well always and everywhere to give you thanks through your beloved son Jesus Christ." The Preface, the opening moment of the Eucharistic Prayer, is a New Testament application of the praise of God in the psalms. The Preface is thanksgiving and praise of God in Christ.

The liturgy has many Prefaces for use according to different circumstances. Each of us could think how our own Preface would be if we had to compose one. It is truly right and fitting, and beautiful for me to worship and praise you, God our Father, through Christ my Lord, through Christ who has called me to faith in my baptism, through Christ who has guided me until now.

Finally, let us consider the Christian instruments of praise. First of all, the human body by which, as Paul says in his Letter to the Romans, we give spiritual worship to God (Romans 12:1). We do this starting with our body: with our mouth, our hands, the things we do and make with our hands. Everything we do in our work can become an instrument of praise. But it starts with ourselves, consecrated instruments adapted for praise through baptism and confirmation, which make us able to praise God in a body which, sanctified by the presence of the Eucharist, can in Christ produce the perfection of praise.

Everyone praises God

Let us look at the Christian reading of the final words of the psalm: "Let everything that breathes praise the Lord."

Every human being is made for the praise of God. Even those who at this moment are not thinking of it, even those who seem far from a state of praise, are in reality made for it.

Praise expresses the marvel of not being the centre of the universe ourselves. It is joy that there is someone greater than ourselves, who loves us infinitely, someone who loves every person. It is the amazement of which Pope John Paul II spoke so beautifully in his first encyclical: "If this profound process takes place within him through which a person realizes himself to be loved by God, he then bears fruit not only of adoration of God but also of deep wonder at himself... In reality, the name for that deep amazement at man's worth and dignity is the Gospel, that is to say, the Good News. It is also called Christianity." (*Redemptor Hominis* 10). We are each called then to this praise in amazement at oneself before the mystery of God, before the beauty, the newness and the power of the Gospel proclamation.

Some questions

At this point let us ask ourselves a few questions:
– Do the people of today praise God? Can we say that we are easily led to praise and thanksgiving, the two leading themes in the psalms? Or rather do other sentiments alternate in us, typical of people who have lost their sense of God? If we no longer know how to praise nor to pray in sorrow and in suffering, then we develop a senseless rage, or else shut ourselves up in a defeatist scepticism, content with any immediate satisfaction. To the biblical formula of praise and lament, expressive of the human condition seen in God, there correspond anger and scepticism which describe human beings when cut off from God, incapable of praise.

Now the question becomes personal. Do I know how to praise? Do I know how to make a loving choice of God? In order to praise we must choose to go forward, decide that we want to praise, and adopt praise as a fundamental attitude. We must not opt for anger or resignation but the love which praises God working in the world.

– Why should we want to praise God? I certainly want to praise him for you, my reader, as St Paul says, for "you are my letter", that anyone may read to find out how strong the word of God is. I want to praise him for you because you have begun to know and love through these pages, praise him for what you are before God. And then I want to praise him for this immense and tremendous gift of life, for this gift which is such a responsibility, but which is at the same time so exciting.

Remembering that to praise means also to know how to mourn, to weep in pain, let us note that praise arouses in us the capacity to see the full value of things, which brings us to mourn their loss deeply. We are then able to mourn in sorrow and anger over lost opportunities; over useless wars, senseless bloodshed for the sake of prestige; for the violence staining the world; conflicts which could be avoided.

We can mourn in sorrow and in anger arising from the praise which faces up to things realistically, not in a destructive rage which achieves nothing, but in an attitude like that of Jesus. We will then be able to root out evil, to build again, to accept sacrifice, to do charitable works and to undertake social and political projects.

It must not start from petty self-interest or calculation but from that fundamental attitude of praise, and therefore of pained and anguished grief at everything that does not correspond to the loving purpose of God.

– The third question is still more personal. How am I to express this desire to praise? It can take a very simple form. Today I met some handicapped lads who are to be confirmed tomorrow. A priest from Lucca, don Luigi Monza, who died ten years ago, a very simple man but with a deep spirituality, founded a charitable institute for these boys.

A maxim in his writing struck me forcibly: "A smile can hide inner pain."

It is a simple statement but one which can transform many of our relationships. A redeeming smile which hides inner pain is a sign of a soul capable of praising God, going beyond what he may be feeling, in order to find the deeper grounds of his ability to smile at others and make a gesture of kindness and considerateness.

Remembering Pope Paul VI

I would like to end this reflection by remembering a man who knew how to praise: Pope Paul VI. He was a man who, precisely because he was deeply conscious of the suffering and tragedies of human life, knew how to rise to a very high quality of praise. I would like to quote some words from his very fine "Thoughts on dying": which is in some ways his spiritual testament. Thinking of his approaching death he says: "... It seems that the departure must be expressed in a great and simple act of recognition and gratitude. This mortal life is, notwithstanding its labours, its hidden secrets, its sufferings, its fatal frailty, a most beautiful thing, a wonder ever original and moving, an event worthy to be celebrated in joy and glory: life, human life! Not less worthy of exaltation and happy amazement is the framework in which human life is contained: this immense world, mysterious, magnificent; this universe with its thousand forces, thousand laws, thousand beauties, thousand depths. Why have I not studied, explored, admired sufficiently this place in which life unfolds? What unpardonable distraction, what reprehensible superficiality! However, even at the last we should recognize that this world, *qui per Ipsum factus est*, which was made through him, is amazing. With immense admiration, and as I have said, with gratitude I salute you and honour you at my leave-taking; behind life, behind nature and the universe, stands Wisdom, and there too, I will say it in these luminous last moments, there stands Love. This world's scene is the design, still today incomprehensible for the most part, of a Creator God, who calls himself our father in heaven. Thank you, O God, thanksgiving and glory to you, Father."

PART II

The school of the word
Reflections on Psalm 50 [RSV:51]

*I wept at the beauty of your hymns, canticles and psalms, and was
powerfully moved at the sweet sound of your Church's singing.
These sounds flowed into my ears, and the truth streamed into my
heart: so that my feeling of devotion overflowed, and tears ran from
my eyes, and I was happy in them.*

*Who can remain unmoved by the many places in the psalms where
the immense majesty of God, his omnipotence, his inexpressible
holiness, his goodness, his mercy, his other infinite perfections are
so sublimely proclaimed? Who is not similarly stirred by the acts of
thanksgiving for God's blessings, by the humble, trusting prayers for
favours desired, by the cries of repentance of the sinful soul? Who is
not fired with love by the faithful portrait of Christ the redeemer
whose voice is heard in all the psalms, singing, sorrowing, rejoicing
in hope, sighing in distress?*

St Augustine, *Confessions*

Reflections on psalm 50 [RSV:51]

PSALM 50 [RSV:51]

Have mercy on me, O God,
    according to thy steadfast love;
    according to thy abundant mercy
      blot out my transgressions.
Wash me thoroughly from my iniquity,
    and cleanse me from my sin!

For I know my transgressions
    and my sin is ever before me.
Against thee, thee only, have I sinned,
    and done that which is evil in thy sight,
so that thou art justified in thy sentence
    and blameless in thy judgement.
Behold, I was brought forth in iniquity,
    and in sin did my mother conceive me.

Behold, thou desirest truth in the inward being;
    therefore teach me wisdom in my secret heart.
Purge me with hyssop, and I shall be clean;
    wash me, and I will be whiter than snow.
Fill me with joy and gladness;
    let the bones which thou hast broken rejoice.

Hide thy face from my sins,
    and blot out all my iniquities.

Create in me a clean heart, O God,
and put a new and right spirit within me.
Cast me not away from thy presence,
and take not thy holy Spirit from me.
Restore to me the joy of thy salvation,
and uphold me with a willing spirit.

Then I will teach transgressors thy ways,
and sinners will return to thee.
Deliver me from bloodguiltiness, O God,
thou God of my salvation,
and my tongue will sing aloud of thy
deliverance.

O Lord, open thou my lips,
and my mouth shall show forth thy praise.
For thou hast no delight in sacrifice;
were I to give you a burnt offering,
thou wouldst not be pleased.
The sacrifice acceptable to God is a broken spirit;
a broken and contrite heart,
O God, thou wilt not despise.

Do good to Zion in thy good pleasure;
rebuild the walls of Jerusalem,
then wilt thou delight in right sacrifices,
in burnt offerings and whole burnt offerings;
then bulls will be offered on thy altar.

1
The starting point

A reading from the Holy Gospel according to Luke (15:1-10):

Now the tax collectors and sinners were all drawing near to hear him. And the Pharisees and the scribes murmured, saying, "This man receives sinners and eats with them."
So he told them this parable: "What man of you, having a hundred sheep, if he has lost one of them, does not leave the ninety-nine in the wilderness, and go after the one which is lost, until he finds it? And when he has found it, he lays it on his shoulders, rejoicing. And when he comes home, he calls together his friends and his neighbours, saying to them, 'Rejoice with me, for I have found my sheep which was lost.' Just so, I tell you, there will be more joy in heaven over one sinner who repents than over ninety-nine righteous persons who need no repentance.
"Or what woman, having ten silver coins, if she loses one coin, does not light a lamp and sweep the house and seek diligently until she finds it? And when she has found it, she calls together her friends and neighbours, saying, 'Rejoice with me, for I have found the coin which I had lost.' Just so, I tell you, there is joy before the angels of God over one sinner who repents."

Have mercy on me, O God,
    according to thy steadfast love;
according to thy abundant mercy
    blot out my transgressions;
wash me thoroughly from my iniquity,
    and cleanse me from my sin!

Choice of theme

You have accepted the invitation to listen to the Word of God and meditate on it. The theme I propose that we should reflect upon now with the aid of a reading of the *Miserere* psalm might be entitled, "Journey of Reconciliation". There are three points which I should like to emphasize by this choice of theme.

(1) There is a strong connection between social and political reconciliation and conversion of heart. This belief has been growing and we want to deepen it by giving it special attention. There cannot be a true, lasting, stable social and political reconciliation among individuals, peoples or nations, without conversion of heart. So too, there is no conversion of heart – as indeed no Christian way of penance – that does not reach out into social and political reconciliation.

(2) There is an itinerary of penance. Conversion of the heart is no simple precise reality: it has stages which are not to be ignored or by-passed. There is a route-plan made to suit the human heart, and we are invited to start out and follow it.

(3) The Church has a mission to the world. This concerns us and it becomes clearer, taking on more precise outlines, as we go along the way of penance. During this journey we ask God to make us much more open and responsive to the problems of human and world reconciliation.

For all these reasons it has seemed to me important that we should reflect on the way of penance.

The Miserere

Psalm 50 (51 according to Hebrew numbering) has inexhaustible riches. It is the daily prayer of the Church, beginning in Latin: *Miserere mei Deus* (Have mercy on me, Lord).

It is found all through the history of the Church and Christian spirituality. It forms the underlying plan of the *Confessions* of St Augustine. It was loved, meditated and commented on by Gregory the Great. It was the battle cry for Joan of Arc's soldiers. It was closely studied by Martin Luther who wrote unforgettable pages on it. It is the hidden mirror of conscience for the characters of Dostoievsky and is the key to his novels.

This then is the psalm of great men and women of God. Musicians like Bach, Donizetti and others nearer to our time have conveyed it in music. Famous painters have delineated it in wonderful engravings.

It is above all the psalm which accompanied the prayers, tears and sufferings of those many men and women who have found in it comfort and understanding at dark and desperate times in their life.

The *Miserere* is the prayer for men and women of all time. It belongs to the history of humanity, not only to the Hebrew Near East or the Christian civilization of the West. Meditating on it, we enter into the human heart and human history.

We can make our own the prayer of Charles de Foucauld: "O God, I thank you for giving us that divine prayer the *Miserere*". May we say this psalm frequently, make it our prayer often; it is a compendium of all prayer: adoration, love, offering, thanksgiving, repentance, petition. It starts from a consideration of ourselves and the consciousness of our sins and rises finally to contemplation of God by way of our neighbour and prayer for the conversion of all.

The divine initiative

Psalm 50 [RSV:51] starts off with these words:

Have mercy on me, O God,
    according to thy steadfast love;
    according to thy abundant mercy

83

blot out my transgressions.
Wash me thoroughly from my iniquity,
and cleanse me from my sin!

The starting point for the heart's journey of conversion is the divine initiative of mercy. God is always the first to put out a hand. The balance is always swayed on the side of his goodness.

The words often used in English to indicate what we have done wrong – sin, fault – do not adequately render the original language. In fact, in the Hebrew text there are three other words which I would rather read as follows:... cross out my *rebellion*, wash me from all my *discord*, cleanse me, 'get me out of' all my *transgression*." Sin is the fundamental spoiling of a person. It is a distortion, a disharmony, a rebellion, a will to something other than, and opposed to, the designs of God.

To the three words describing human transgression are counterpointed three of the divine names: "Pity... mercy... love". The former are one human sin, however variously called, and the latter are three attributes of God. The disproportion indicates that the emphasis is not on sinful humanity, on the poverty of what we are, but on the infinity of God.

We will try to reflect briefly on these words defining the God of mercy and goodness.

Who is God?

The first word of the Latin *Miserere* we can translate as "*Pity* me, O God". In Hebrew it is simply: "*Grace*, be gracious to me, fill me with your grace."

We ask God then to be *grace* for us, to take an interest in our troubles, and to give us a hand. This is what Mary knew when she sang: "Lord, you have regarded the low estate of your handmaiden and done great things for me, you have filled me with your grace."

God is free gift, the essence of giving. When we say God has no interest in thinking of us, taking notice of us, we show we have the wrong idea of God. To put it in technical terms, we have a Pharisaic idea of God, because we have been calculating in efforts to understand him.

God rejoices in the power to give anything to anyone who needs help, anyone who feels that he is a nobody, anyone who feels down. He wants to pour his strength into us, not judge us.

The second word is *mercy*. It is interesting to note that the expression is: "according to thy abundant mercy" and not "in your mercy" or "because you are merciful". The psalmist underlines the infinite extent of the divine mercy, which we sense without understanding.

In Hebrew the term is *hesed* and it has a long history rich in meaning. It indicates God's typical attitude towards his people, which includes loyalty, trustworthiness, faithfulness, goodness, tenderness, considerateness, constancy and love.

It could also be translated as "loving kindness" with the sense of tender affection, one who will not play false, or leave us in the lurch.

God is the one I do not know but for whom I am important. For him – as Jesus himself said – every hair of my head is important. Nothing happens to me without God's tender attention.

We translate *hesed* by "mercy" because God's kindness is more tender when we are weak, frail, sinful, inconstant, sulky, unattractive and especially when we hope not to be noticed by God for fear of being punished.

The third phrase is "according to thy steadfast love." In Hebrew it is *rahammim* and means "*the heart*, or the viscera". It is a profoundly maternal word and indicates the capacity to carry something within, to immerse oneself in a situation to such an extent as to live it in one's own flesh, to suffer or rejoice, as the case may be.

This attribute of God is something a person who has loved another creature with a total love can understand. Such love is visceral and passionate. We might almost translate: "according to your great passion for humanity, have mercy, O God."

These three attributes of God set the tone of Psalm 50 [51], which is a hymn about encountering God as he is. Starting out from contemplation of the divine initiative towards humanity, it invites us to have above all a great and true idea of God.

Personal questions

Let us ask ourselves some questions:

– First question: Do I have a right idea of God? Do I know him as he is? This first question is important because anyone who does not have a right idea of God has no right idea of himself or herself, or of others.

In chapter 15 of St Luke's Gospel, we read that "the Pharisees and the scribes murmured" at Jesus because he received sinners and ate with them (see Luke 15:1-10). That shows the typical attitude of one who does not have a right idea of God, who thinks of God as vengeful, touchy or peevish. Often, by not accepting ourselves, we come to believe that God does not accept us entirely. It is true that at times we make a show of great self-assurance, bravado almost, asserting that we have no need of God. However, at other times there rises up in us that profound insecurity which is at the heart of every person and is a mark of our creatureliness. In the religious context that is expressed almost with the fear of a rather nasty God, a God who does not do me justice, who demands too much of me, who has put me in difficult circumstances, or who is too difficult himself and is unapproachable.

Behind all these sentiments there is probably the conviction that God does not love me as I am and that he is not pleased with me.

The great revelation in Psalm 50 [51] is that on the contrary God does love me as I am, accepts me entirely, and for that reason he is good, courteous, considerate, attentive and kind to me.

All this was well understood by the shepherd in the parable in St Luke where we read: "When he has found it (the lost sheep), he lays it on his shoulders, *rejoicing*. And when he comes home, he calls together his friends and his neighbours, saying to them: 'Rejoice with me, for I have found my sheep which was lost'" (Luke 15:5-6). The woman who had lost her drachma understood it too when, on finding it, she called her friends in and said: "Rejoice with me" (Luke 15:9).

Jesus ends the parable: "Just so, I tell you, there is joy among the angels of God over one sinner who repents" (Luke 15:10).

Each of us ought to be able to say: God rejoices in me, he is happy about me, I am somebody very important to him.

To have a just idea of God then is to start off on the right foot on the road to reconciliation.

– Second question: Do I have a wrong idea of God?

We have already said that the Pharisees and scribes who murmured against Jesus had a wrong idea of God.

Does some deep grievance vex us frequently, which we dare not tell anyone and of which we are ashamed?

Do we rebel against God, do we have some secret resentment against him?

– Third question: What can I do to correct my wrong idea of God?

One way certainly is to listen to his Word through a prayerful reading of the Scriptures which bring the often repressed feelings to light in an expression of God's praise. I will try then to interpret the words of the psalm: "Give me grace, O God, according to your great passion for humanity. In your loving kindness cancel the wrong idea I have of you! I am sorry, Father, that I have entertained it. You alone can give me the right idea, because how can I know you if you do not reveal yourself, and if your Son does not awaken in me the knowledge of you?"

– Finally: Do I have a wrong idea of my neighbour? What can I do to correct it?

The wrong idea I can have of God might contribute to a wrong idea of my neighbour. This happens not when we criticize, because sometimes our neighbour is at fault (we all know something of that!), but when we constantly complain about someone, when a person or a situation does not suit us. It then becomes obvious that we have not adopted the right attitude, the one that God has towards us, which is comprehensive, loving and positive.

Often we set up emotional blocks against people, and then everything they do is wrong. At times our confessions are a list of grievances about others. If we had a right idea of God, it would then make us see the defects of others in a new light, as God does with us.

Why do we not imitate God and take a lesson from him? Instead of forever asking ourselves why the other person has treated me badly, let us try asking: What can I do for the other person? How can I change that person's heart?

2
Identifying the situation

A reading from the Holy Gospel according to Luke
(15:11-32)

And he said, "There was a man who had two sons; and the younger of them said to his father, 'Father, give me the share of property that falls to me.' And he divided his living between them. Not many days later, the younger son gathered all he had and took his journey into a far country, and there he squandered his property in loose living. And when he had spent everything, a great famine arose in that country, and he began to be in want. So he went and joined himself to one of the citizens of that country, who sent him into his fields to feed swine. And he would gladly have fed on the pods that the swine ate; and no one gave him anything. But when he came to himself he said, 'How many of my father's hired servants have bread enough and to spare, but I perish here with hunger! I will arise and go to my father, and I will say to him, "Father, I have sinned against heaven and before you; I am no longer worthy to be called your son; treat me as one of your hired servants."' And he arose and came to his father. But while he was yet at a distance, his father saw him and had compassion, and ran and embraced him, 'Father, I have sinned against heaven and before you; I am no longer worthy to be called your son.' But the father said to his servants, 'Bring quickly the best robe, and put it on him; and put a ring on his hand, and shoes on his feet; and bring the fatted calf and kill it, and let us eat and make merry; for this my son was dead, and is alive again; he was lost, and is found.' And they began to make merry.

"Now his elder son was in the field; and as he came and drew near to the house, he heard music and dancing.

And he called one of the servants and asked what this meant. And he said to him, 'Your brother has come, and your father has killed the fatted calf, because he has received him safe and sound.' But he was angry and refused to go in. His father came out and entreated him, but he answered his father, 'Lo, these many years I have served you, and I never disobeyed your command; yet you never gave me a kid, that I might make merry with my friends. But when this son of yours came, who has devoured your living with harlots, you killed for him the fatted calf!" And he said to him, 'Son, you are always with me, and all that is mine is yours. It was fitting to make merry and be glad, for this your brother was dead, and is alive; he was lost, and is found.'"

For I know my transgressions
    and my sin is ever before me.
Against thee, thee only, have I sinned,
    and done that which is evil in thy sight,

Behold, I was brought forth in iniquity,
    and in sin did my mother conceive me.
Behold, thou desirest truth in the inward being;
    therefore teach me wisdom in my secret heart.

The first lines of the psalm with which we are concerned introduce us to the central section, which can conveniently be divided into three parts.

The first part identifies the situation. The verbs are all in the indicative, stating and underlining facts: I know my transgressions, against thee have I sinned, thou art justified in thy sentence.

The second part expresses supplication. The passage changes in tone and almost all the verbs are in the imperative: teach me wisdom, purge me, wash me, fill me with joy, hide thy face, restore to me the joy of thy salvation, uphold me.

The third part looks into the future. The verbs are in the future tense: I will teach, my tongue will sing aloud.

In terms more familiar to us we can call the three parts: (1) the examination of conscience – identifying the situation; (2) request for absolution – petition; (3) resolution – plan for the future. These are three periods in the reading clearly differentiated if only by the difference in the verbs.

Towards the truth about ourselves

Three subjects of the verbs are shown in action.

The most frequent subject to appear is myself, the *I*. *I* know my transgressions, against thee have *I* sinned, and done that which is evil.

Another subject, in the third person, is *sin*. It is the reality of sin which confronts this man. I was brought forth in iniquity, in *sin* did my mother conceive me.

The third subject in action, the principal one, the key to understanding the whole passage is: *thou*.

There is, then, the *I* which identifies; there is a general reference to the state of *sin*; there is the *thou* with which this first part ends and which is the focal point: *Thou* desirest truth in the inward being, therefore teach me wisdom.

Let us try to reflect first of all on the phrases which have "thou" as subject so that we can understand better what goes before.

In the Hebrew text the expression "thou desirest truth in the inmost being" is a little difficult: "Thou lovest truth in the dark", that is, you love the truth which is light even where a person is lost in the labyrinth of conscience.

"Teach me wisdom in my secret heart." Wisdom is one of the loftiest and most profound realities in the Old Testament. It is order, proportion, light, creative warmth, the divine plan of salvation.

Here is the key to the first part of the psalm. God, in his loving initiative, projects into the dark of my psyche, into the depths of my conscience, the light of his plan. By doing that he enables me to discover the truth of myself, gives me pause, helps me to understand myself in regard to what I am

91

called to be, to what I should have been, to what I can be with his grace.

The truth and wisdom of God are a true, friendly, beneficent light which, entering into the depths of the soul where not even I myself can account for what is going on, instructs me and leads me to the true knowledge of myself.

Dialogue with the thou

If we have grasped, at least a little, the force of these words, we can make a better reading of what comes at the beginning: "Against thee, thee only, have I sinned": I have done what is wrong in your eyes.

At first sight this expression appears strange, especially if we refer it to David who, historically, epitomizes the happening recounted in the psalm. David sinned not just against God but also against his friend whose death he treacherously engineered. So he was both betrayer and murderer.

Yet the emphasis is on the relationship with God which resulted from these actions. No one in fact knew about David's sin, so successful was the plot he had woven, and Nathan was the only one to reproach him. However, when the horror of the scheme he had carried out was brought home to him, David was faced with the torture of a guilty conscience.

In sinning against a friend by betrayal, unfaithfulness and adultery, David had set himself against God and against all those whom God champions as his own: "Against thee, thee only, have I sinned." The expression is very similar to the central words of the Gospel parable of the Prodigal Son: "Father, I have sinned against heaven and before you." Everything the son had done was concerned with other things: his dissolute life, his squandering, mistakes and excesses. All that however is placed within the framework of his relationship with God (see Luke 15:11-32).

A person taught by God enters deep into the truth of

himself or herself, and recognizes that their wrong-doing, whether small or great, has marred God's image and ruined their relationship with God.

This reproof is important for us, who are accustomed today to emphasize the social aspects of sin which naturally is not only against God, but also against the Church, society and community. Here, we are reminded that God stands behind every person we treat badly or deceive, or undervalue. We set ourselves against God every time we reject our brother or sister, who expects from us an act of charity or justice. All the problems of family relationships, problems between individuals and problems in society are our own problems in dialogue with the One who loves us, knows us and helps us to know ourselves in the light of his truth.

It does not in fact say in the psalm: I have sinned. It says:"Against thee have I sinned". To accept responsibility for a fault is always an act of profound truth and an extremely pure act because this admission has nothing to do with an abasing, humiliating sense of guilt.

We are all subject to times of inescapable sadness, anger, indignation and waging war on ourselves. The suffering caused by a sense of guilt which has not been taken into dialogue with God cannot improve us in any way.

The words of the psalm reveal the difference between an examination of conscience made in dialogue with God and an analysis of our faults and weaknesses, which profoundly depress our spirit, making it still weaker in the struggle against sin.

In this psalm, written more than two thousand years ago, we can see a man who has found justification through repentance, the way of acknowledging the gravest of faults before the One who changes the hearts. We note also the personal, emotive character of the words: "What is evil in thy sight": in your eyes – despite the love with which you have created me and sustained me.

How different this is from the so-called legal regrets. An apology in a court of law can certainly produce edifying advantages through the settlement it brings about but it does not have the power to purify the conscience from the harm done. The repentant person will still have to say: my sin is always before me, unless of course he or she enters into that mysterious process of transformation of the human heart: "Create in me a clean heart, O God." We are transformed and renewed solely by the power of God.

Personal questions

We have seen that the examination of conscience means allowing God to show us the truth about ourselves. The words of the psalm can renew in us the religious sense, which perhaps has been atrophied through meaningless repetitive acts.

I now suggest two very simple questions in preparation for the Sacrament of Reconciliation.

– What things would I rather not have on my conscience? What is weighing on me, defiling me, oppressing me, making me what I do not want to be? Let us allow what emerges in reply to this question to be expressed simply, without immediate recourse to ready formulas. This is indeed the truth of ourselves manifested as a prayer, a desire, a true or a spoiled self-portrait.

– What would I have liked to be? How would I have liked to behave in the situations which are weighing on me?

This is where the dialogue begins to clarify motives and judgements, renewing us from within in that creative process praised in the second part of the psalm, on which we shall meditate in a later chapter.

After these questions, I suggest four reflections:

– When was the last time I made an examination of conscience?

– Does examination of conscience bore me, disturb me or leave me happy?

To understand better the point of this question it may help you to read the following passage from the autobiography of St Ignatius Loyola: When thinking about things of the world he felt much pleasure (the saint writes in the third person, though speaking of himself), but when, wearied of it, he desisted, he felt empty and dejected. On the other hand, while journeying barefoot to Jerusalem, eating only herbs, practising all the austerity he imagined the saints did, there were thoughts that not only consoled him in the midst of his sufferings, but also left him satisfied and full of joy even after they had ceased. At the time he gave no attention to this and did not stop to consider the difference. Then one occasion opened his eyes; and he marvelled at that difference and began considering; from this experience he deduced that some thoughts left him sad, others happy, and gradually he came to recognize the spirits which moved him: the one of the demon, the other of God.

It is therefore important to ask oneself whether the exercise of the examination of conscience is a burden or whether it leaves us content.

— Do I think of the examination of conscience as the divine invitation to dialogue, that is, a conversation with a "thou"? Or rather do I make of it a punctilious, wearing, psychological analysis? Do I usually think of it as a dialogue in which I speak, listen, express myself trustfully with the joy of being welcomed, accepted for what I am, and restored?

— If I find difficulty in the examination of conscience, an unavoidable task for anyone wanting self-knowledge, do I let myself be helped by the Church in the dialogue of penance?

The 1983 Synod of Bishops spoke at length of the journey to conversion necessary for every individual and every community. They also spoke of the stages in this journey, one to gain the ability for authentic recognition of what we are and for giving a clear account to the person who, in God's name, listens to us in a fatherly dialogue.

The Lord is quick to transform our life if we put it in his hands and I would wish you to have this experience, which will be one of the most beautiful in your life.

3
Sorrow for sin

A reading from the Holy Gospel according to Luke
(22:54-62):

Then they seized him and led him away, bringing him
away, bringing him into the high priest's house. Peter
followed at a distance; and when they had kindled a fire
in the middle of the courtyard and sat down together,
Peter sat among them. Then a maid, seeing him as he sat
in the light and gazing at him, said, "This man also was
with him." But he denied it, saying, "Woman, I do not
know him." And a little later someone else saw him and
said, "You also are one of them." But Peter said, "Man,
I am not." And after an interval of about an hour still
another insisted, saying, "Certainly this man also was
with him; for he is a Galilean." But Peter said, "Man, I do
not know what you are saying." And immediately, while
he was still speaking, the cock crowed. And the Lord
turned and looked at Peter. And Peter remembered the
word of the Lord, how he had said to him, "Before the
cock crows today, you will deny me three times." And he
went out and wept bitterly.

Thou art justified in thy sentence
and blameless in thy judgement.

To complete our reflection on the first part of the central
section of Psalm 50 [51], let us meditate on the words: "Thou

art justified in thy sentence and blameless in thy judgement."
This will help us to begin our reflections on sorrow for sin.

The word "sorrow" as used in the context of the Sacrament of Reconciliation can arouse in us a feeling of uneasiness or dissatisfaction.

It is a reminder of emotions at times squeezed dry; of the uncertainty we may feel whether we have been truly sorry in a particular confession and perhaps for this reason put off confession.

And yet in the area of physical experience, pain and suffering are the most evident and the least artificial of feelings. I feel pain physically whether I want to or not. In the same way mental suffering is something very real.

What then is this sorrow for sin which seems to have little in common with the feeling of physical or mental pain?

Self-evaluation

There are things, more or less serious, which each of us would rather not have done: ways of acting, responding, proceeding which, though not quite obvious, fail to live up to the image we have of ourselves.

At times, we notice, such things do not even depend on ourselves; rather they are governed by previous habits or oversights. All the same we feel that they are nothing to boast of.

This capacity for self-judgement is not sorrow for sin, but it does lead to it. In fact I can only repent of something which I myself have done. I did it and I don't approve of it.

The way of Christian purification presupposes the capacity for self-judgement and implies dissociating ourselves from things those of which we do not approve.

To be able to do this is a sign of freedom of action, a sign of human and moral maturity. There is cause for doubt if a person is always accusing others and justifying himself in everything. If in our confessions we always come round to accusing others and excusing ourselves, we show we have not taken even the first step towards Christian repentance.

On the other hand it is true that, perhaps through a certain habit of the Sacrament of Penance, our repentance is sometimes blocked by the fact that we are not convinced of the necessity of blaming ourselves for everything in us that we don't like. We don't feel like admitting that the fault is always ours.

More often repentance is blocked because we are not convinced that what we have done should not have been done. Maybe tradition and doctrine say we are wrong but secretly we feel that it is not so. In this case, repentance becomes difficult, superficial or artificial.

What ought we to do if we find that our repentance does not flow freely due to our failure to give a true assessment of ourselves?

Clearly the way to go about it is to pass from a hasty estimation of ourselves to a more realistic and balanced evaluation by reflection and prayer.

Instead of beginning straight out with the confession proper, it might be a good thing to talk simply and in friendly fashion, which would allow us to express the problem clearly and to seek help in dealing with it. This would be more sensible than dwelling on the problem and letting ourselves be hypnotized by it.

With these three considerations, we are still at the beginning of what Christian sorrow for sin is. It rises and takes shape at a higher level of consciousness and we try to understand it by meditating on the words of Psalm 50 [51].

The injured party

"So that thou art justified in thy sentence and blameless in thy judgement?" What does it mean exactly? We spontaneously interpret these lines by putting God in the position of judge. In our mind's eye we see two parties who have gone to arbitration, and God in the middle.

The two parties in the case of the psalm's historical context are David and Uriah, Beersheba's husband who was treacherously killed at David's orders. God stands between them as an impartial judge who condemns David. The king accepts the judgement and then says to God: you are blameless when you judge.

This interpretation does not fit. It makes God an arbiter who condemns the sinner to death without possibility of appeal.

The reality as seen in the psalm is much more profound.

God is not the judge: he is the injured party. He, the principle of all fidelity and all love, has been injured by David. For this he reproaches David who accepts the rebuke knowing that the divine judgement is just. He also knows that this judgement brings pardon with it.

God, as the offended party, reproves David because he wants him to live and not die. David has thought of killing God: God wants to save him.

It is precisely at this point that biblical repentance appears as the sorrow of humankind. Humanity finds itself before the One it has injured, whose faithfulness it has rejected, and who again offers it the right hand of fidelity.

If we wonder how an offence against our neighbour affects and hurts God, he himself will answer with the vision of the Burning Bush from the Book of Exodus. Pharaoh was oppressing the Hebrews and God, appearing to Moses, constitutes himself the injured party and starts his action against the oppressor with these words: "I have seen the affliction of *my* people who are in Egypt, and have heard their cry because of their taskmasters; I know their sufferings, and I have come down to deliver them" (Exodus 3:7,8).

He will answer also in the Gospel of Matthew with the scene of the Last Judgement where Jesus claims to be the injured party whenever a starving person is not fed and a prisoner not visited: "Truly I say to you... you did it not to me" (see Matthew 25:31-46).

Peter's tears

There is a passage in the Gospel of Luke which can give you a deeper experience of the sorrow for sin which we have been meditating on in the words of David. It is the episode where Peter denies Jesus three times: "And immediately, while he was still speaking, the cock crowed. And the Lord turned and looked at Peter. And Peter remembered the word of the Lord, how he had said to him, 'Before the cock crows today, you will deny me three times.' And he went out and wept bitterly" (Luke 22:54-62).

Why did Peter burst into tears?

Up to that point he had a hazy knowledge of having done wrong, of having dishonoured himself by betraying a friend.

But it is only when Jesus meets him and looks at him, that Peter bursts into tears. At that moment he knows only one thing: I have denied this man, and he is going to die for me!

It is the unbelievable superabundance of trust and consideration shown to one who has forfeited them which brings out the contrast. Christian sorrow for sin springs from seeing this contrast, from the encounter with the One who, when offered an insult to himself and to his love for humanity, offers in return a look of friendship.

We may think that something similar must have happened in the conscience of the man who attempted to assassinate John Paul II, when the Pope went unarmed into his cell, bent over him full of sympathy listened to him as a friend.

Such experiences cannot be described but can only be grasped intuitively by each one of us.

Personal questions

The revelation of guilt comes to a Christian when he meets Christ in his Word and in himself. This meeting changes our rigid judgement of ourselves, a judgement which is always unsafe and clumsy, into true repentance and inward grief at having offended Christ himself. We experience grief for spoiling our relationship as friends, for breaking the code of honour and affection, for neglecting and damaging a precious relationship.

We can ask ourselves:

– "Against you, against you only have I sinned" What comes to mind when I reflect on these words?

– Often I refuse to pay attention, listen, help or show esteem for others. Have I grasped the connection between harm done to another and harm done to my friendship and union with God which began in baptism and continues in the eucharistic life?

– Do I realize the restorative power of forgiveness? I too, like Jesus, can forgive, bring to life, and give back faith and honour.

Shall I manage to do so? Do I call on the Holy Spirit to spread around me the power of Christ's reconciliation?

And we can say:

Grant us, Lord, to seek the path of repentance and enter the right way so that our starting out may not only be for ourselves, but for all those who are on the way to a change of heart. And may you, Lord, who gave David and Peter sorrow for sin, grant deep sorrow to us for having offended you.

4

Supplication

A reading from the Holy Gospel according to John (8:2-11):

Early in the morning he came again to the temple; all the people came to him, and he sat down and taught them. The scribes and the Pharisees brought a woman who had been caught in adultery, and placing her in the midst they said to him, "Teacher, this woman has been caught in the act of adultery. Now in the law Moses commanded us to stone such. What do you say about her?" This they said to test him, that they might have some charge to bring against him. Jesus bent down and wrote with his finger on the ground. And as they continued to ask him he stood up and said to them, "Let him who is without sin among you be the first to throw a stone at her." And once more he bent down to write with his finger on the ground. But when they heard it, they went away, one by one, beginning with the eldest, and Jesus was left alone with the woman standing before him. Jesus looked up and said to her, "Woman, where are they? Has no one condemned you?" She said, "No one, Lord." And Jesus said, "Neither do I condemn you; go, and do not sin again."

> Create in me a clean heart, O God,
>   and put a new and right spirit within me.
> Cast me not away from thy presence,
>   and take not thy holy Spirit from me.
> Restore to me the joy of thy salvation,
>   and uphold me with a willing spirit.

The words composing the second part of the psalm are words of supplication, invocation, prayer. They express the authentic entreaty of one who knows God and is beginning to know himself. Let us ask the Lord for the grace to be able to do the same.

Invocation of the Spirit

Let us begin with a linguistic detail which does not show up in the translation. We have before us three invocations or requests from humanity to the Holy Spirit. The line translated by "uphold me with a willing spirit" in fact reads in the Hebrew text: "strengthen me with your generous Spirit", or "put a generous Spirit within me."

The petition asks for the steadfast Spirit, the Holy Spirit, the generous Spirit, and is a true and proper *epiclesis* or invocation.

The liturgical *epiclesis* is the prayer in the Mass at the time of the consecration calling on the Holy Spirit to descend in a creative way upon the bread and wine, making them the Body and Blood of Christ.

Besides this eucharistic invocation of the Spirit, the liturgy has in some of the prayers of the Canon a communal *epiclesis* in which the Holy Spirit is asked to descend on those present and make them one in Christ.

Here, we have a penitential *epiclesis*, an invocation of the Spirit to descend on the one praying and transform that person. It is therefore the culminating point of the psalm, as the consecration is the culmination of the Eucharist.

A new creation

Let us now reflect on two parallel requests: "Create in me a clean heart, O God" is at the beginning of the *epiclesis* of the Spirit, and the other, "Restore to me the joy of thy salvation" at the end.

Which is the fundamental petition? "Create in me."

The verb "to create" is the first in Scripture: "In the beginning God *created* heaven and earth" (Genesis 1:1). It is a word the Bible reserves for God alone and never used for any human action. It is exclusively the divine act bringing things into being out of nothing.

This petition is, then, for a creative act, for something new which God alone can bring about in a person.

And the phrase "create in me" is parallel with the other: "restore to me the joy…" In the Hebrew it reads: "Make joy return to me, revive in me." It is not asking for something entirely new but for a return of that original creative moment which is baptism.

The Sacrament of Reconciliation is a request to be plunged again in the creative power of the baptismal Spirit, a fresh experience of baptism, which we have lost through our fault.

For this reason the Sacrament of Reconciliation cannot have its full effect if we have not experienced deeply the proclamation of the Gospel, the power of the *kerygma*.

How can something be restored which has never been there, or which was there only in a vague and colourless state?

How is it possible to retrieve the power of baptism if it has never been accepted in a genuine, personal commitment?

Penitential conversion should enable us to find again the power of baptism, which some may perhaps have never experienced because they have never made the gift of themselves to God. That gift which we are called to make in the Eucharist, in Confirmation or in a spiritual retreat can lead us to understand the power of God's saving message.

Without that primary experience, confession cannot be a new act of God leading a person back into the fullness of the Holy Spirit bestowed in Baptism and Confirmation.

Christian joy

What is the object of the creative, restorative act which God is called upon to fulfil? It is a pure heart, it is joy.

Scripture shows joy as the fundamental Christian experience corresponding to a clean heart. It is a heart without reproach because it has been made welcome and completely restored by God the loving Father.

Joy is the fundamental experience which we should have in us. And yet so often when we think about our Christian life, we have to see it as a life which drags on wearily. Not because there is no joy in us – there is the power of the Holy Spirit in us indeed and we all have it – but because we don't express it, or open our lives to it, and so it remains almost imperceptible.

The time for joy is the time of prayer, adoration, silence, song, discussion of the Gospel. It is the moment of sacrifice, the gift of self, renunciation; it is the moment of interior song. At those times, joy which is not ours but the gift of God, breaks out in us and takes us by surprise.

"Create in me a clean heart, O God... give me back the joy of being saved." It is God's saving joy which welcomes me, helps me, saves me.

It is the joy of the adulterous woman spoken about in the Gospel of John (8:2-11). This passage is not to be found in many of the Gospel manuscripts, yet this refreshing episode has been part of the early Christian catechesis. It is not there probably because it was considered dangerous, the adulterous woman's effort at repentance not being sufficiently clear. It seems a passage condoning wrong-doing. And yet those who read it in that sense and then removed it from many manuscripts and codices of Scripture did not understand the creative pardon of God, the renewing power of his spirit in the heart of a person. They did not understand God's ability to make a new person, not as a result of human good will only but mainly through the creative power of the Spirit.

The woman hardly expressing her joy in words is a figure of each one of us saved by a forgiving word of Christ.

Certainty of pardon

To say that God will certainly forgive us is not simply placing a bet on our future. It is not a forecast of what we shall be. Nor is it a guarantee of success in fully mastering ourselves.

If God loves me and forgives me, I can say to him: "Lord, make me different! You know that I want to be better than what I am!"

Our certainty of pardon derives from this appeal, which gradually makes room in our heart for joy and the strength of the Spirit. It is St Augustine's experience:

> But you, Lord, had regard to the deep death that was in me and drew out the abyss of corruption that was in the bottom of my heart... How lovely I suddenly found it, to be free from those empty vanities which at first I had been so afraid to put aside, yet now it was a joy to dismiss them!
>
> In truth it was you who cast them out of me, you, supreme loveliness. You cast them out and you took their place in me, you sweeter than any pleasure; brighter than all light yet more intimate than any secret; more sublime than any honours but not to those sublime in their own eyes.
>
> Now my spirit was free of the gnawing cares of ambition, gain and voluptuousness, scab of restless libidinous passion, and I talked familiarly with you my light, my riches and my salvation, O Lord, my God (*Confessions* IX 1).

Personal reflections

I suggest three questions for you to consider:
– Do I believe that God can create a pure heart in me or do I live resigned to my weakness, telling myself there is nothing to be done because that is how I am made?

Have I faith in the power of the Spirit recreated in me through Baptism and the Sacrament of Reconciliation? Here we can pray: "Lord, increase my faith. It is weak and so I am always the same. I resign myself too easily to being what I am, while you are calling me to accept that I am loved by you and called by you to something which deep down I desire."

– Do I believe that God can create hearts anew?

This question is concerned with the way I look at others. I often look at them as incorrigible and their actions as inevitable, and I do nothing to help them because I have no faith in the creative power of the Spirit.

I always complain of others, but I don't pray for them. I say I have been wronged and think that, while I can be converted, there is no conversion for them.

– Do I open up to the joy of being saved? Do I let it express itself? When may it express itself in me?

Perhaps it is expressed at a time of silent daily reflection on a page of the Gospel; perhaps on resolutely facing up to a sacrifice; perhaps in a friendly word of forgiveness.

Let us pray for one another that our hearts may open up to the joy of salvation which comes from the Lord, joy in what God is working in us. Let us pray that hearts can believe in the divine power of salvation and can have the patience and love to be instruments of this power of salvation.

5
Confession of sins

A reading from the Holy Gospel according to Luke (18:9-14):

> He also told this parable to some who trusted in themselves that they were righteous and despised others: "Two men went up into the temple to pray, one a Pharisee and the other a tax collector. The Pharisee stood and prayed thus with himself, 'God, I thank thee that I am not like other men, extortioners, unjust, adulterers, or even like this tax collector. I fast twice a week, I give tithes of all that I get.' But the tax collector, standing far off, would not even lift up his eyes to heaven, but beat his breast, saying, 'God, be merciful to me a sinner!' I tell you, this man went down to his house justified rather than the other; for every one who exalts himself will be humbled, but he who humbles himself will be exalted."

And done that which is evil in thy sight.

At this point in our reflections on Psalm 50 [51] we are able to understand better what "confession" really is.

It is a very important subject for our journey of reconciliation. On the other hand, the acknowledgement of sins which the penitent is obliged to make before the Church always arouses an uneasy feeling and poses various questions.

Let us try first to pinpoint the unease and the questions.

Uneasiness about the *content* of the confession. It is not unusual for us to feel embarrassment at not knowing what to say. Let us turn to the priest then and say: "Could you help me, please, I don't know what I have to say."

Sometimes we don't know how to express ourselves: "Please help me because I don't know how to put it, I am confused. I've something weighing on me but I don't quite know how to say it."

Uneasiness can also arise from the *form* of confession, or the atmosphere surrounding it. It can easily become a detailed self-accusation: I committed this, I did that, I am guilty of the other.

In a more psychological frame of reference, the acknowledgement of sins turns into a self-analysis which risks turning into self-justification. I am very self-critical and succeed so well in explaining myself to myself that in practice I don't really need pardon from God: the forgiveness becomes secondary. In fact the Gospel on forgiveness is almost repudiated.

Or the opposite can happen – self-flagellation. Here we accuse ourselves endlessly, with a stubborn harshness towards ourselves which is a sign of a flawed understanding of confession.

Questions about *values* then arise. What use is confession? What positive use has it for the personality? Why is it necessary to go to confession? Would it not be better to let each one say interiorly, in a general way: I have sinned?

Or is it not better to acknowledge it by a gesture, striking the breast, without bothering to make a detailed and tiresome confession?

Content of confession

In our considerations we have been guided by line 6 of Psalm 50 [51] which we have already meditated upon and which says: "[I] have done that which is evil in thy sight."

The first thing we notice from this phrase is that it is part of a dialogue. This is not self-criticism: I have done the wrong thing, I have done as I ought not, I have made a blunder.

Rather we are in an intimate and personal dialogue here: I have done what is wrong in your eyes. I have done wrong not only against your law but what is bad "in thy sight".

We are not in the area of self-accusation or self-flagellation. This is a dialogue with One who loves us.

Yet the dialogue remains general. It is generalized in the same way as the other expressions in the psalm. I recognize my fault (which fault?); my sin is always before me (what sin?); against you, against you alone have I sinned.

The *Miserere*, strangely, does not specify the actual sin committed, which makes us ask: is that necessary? Is there any point in going further into it?

We cannot stop at this generalized declaration, which is basically also that of the publican in the Gospel: "O God, have mercy on me a sinner."

In other passages Sacred Scripture gives us examples of less general confessions. In the ninth chapter of the Book of Ezra, we see that, starting from a particular sin concerning the social customs of the people of Israel, there is, first, an acknowledgement. Having profaned the holy race by mixing with the local population, the magistrates and chieftains had been the first to admit their infidelity. Then comes the confession prayer: "I fell upon my knees and spread out my hands to the Lord my God, saying: 'O my God, I am ashamed and blush to lift my face to thee, my God, for our iniquities have risen higher than our heads'" (Ezra 9:5-6). Here we have expressed all the consequences of the fault, and finally there is taken up again the specific description of what has happened: "We have forsaken thy commandments which thou didst command by thy servants the prophets saying, 'The land which you are entering, to take possession of it, is a land unclean... We have not obeyed thy commandments of purity, yet thou, our God, hast punished us less than our iniquities deserved'" (see Ezra 9:10ff).

It is worth examining in detail this case of a specific confession of what has happened and the repentance that follows.

We find another well-known confession of the specific

rebellion of Israel in the ninth chapter of the Book of Ne-hemiah: "Thou art a God ready to forgive... Even when they had made for themselves a molten calf and said, 'This is your God who brought you up out of Egypt,' and had committed great blasphemies, thou in thy great mercies didst not forsake them in the wilderness" (9:17-19).

There are then in Scripture, here and elsewhere, examples of confessions where the acknowledgement expresses the actual feelings of the one guilty before God.

If we return to Psalm 50 [51] after reflecting on these examples and read it in the context of its positioning in the psalter we realize that here too we have before us a well-defined and specific confession, which is a continuation of the theme in the preceding psalm, which with Psalm 50 [51] appears to constitute a liturgical whole.

Psalms 49 [50] and 50 [51] were in fact a penitential liturgy which began with a circumstantial indictment on the part of God and the acceptance of that accusation by the penitent. Let us read the charge which God makes in Psalm 49 [50]:18ff:

> If you see a thief, you are a friend of his;
>   and you keep company with adulterers.
> You give your mouth free rein for evil,
>   and your tongue frames deceit.
> You sit and speak against your brother;
>   you slander your own mother's son.
> These things you have done and I
>   have been silent...

And then follows the prayer:

> Purge me with hyssop, and I shall be clean;
>   wash me, and I will be whiter than snow.
> Fill me with joy and gladness ...

From all these words of Scripture we can understand that it is the Word of God reproaching the penitent and questioning him on his sin.

The examination of conscience – we can understand it better now – is putting oneself before the Word of God which transcends the ethical frame of reference in order to question and chide in love, eliciting the spark of salvation and the possibility of pardon.

The content of the confession is not a groping for something to say. It is not a wearisome account, as if there was "something wrong inside". It is a response to the questioning by the Word of God which also enlightens.

By letting ourselves be questioned and reproved by the Word, we put ourselves in a position to confess humbly, simply and clearly: Yes, Lord, it's true: you are right, but you create a new heart in me!

Obviously this does not mean that an acknowledgement of faults must always refer directly to some passage in the Gospel. It is a response to God who turns to us with his power and love. God loves us and for this reason he does not flatter us nor deceive us with empty words or vague consolations; but he interrogates us with the power of Scripture, the Magisterium of the Church, the words of those who love us and speak in his name.

The process of changing a person is not raging against fictitious sins or unassailable attitudes. It is placing oneself in the framework of the Covenant and recognizing that the Covenant as God's summons often finds us wanting in the dialogue of love, and calls for a dialogue of repentance and reconciliation.

The background to confession

If we read Psalms 49 [50] and 50 [51], which we have put together into a liturgical unit, we notice that the Hebrew root to which reference is made to indicate confession, is a word which perhaps some of us can recall.

Indeed, anyone who has been in the Holy Land has certainly heard often the word *toda* or *todarabba* which means "thank you".

In Israel every time a favour is asked or a purchase is made, the reply is *toda*, thank you; *todarabba*, thank you very much.

This is the key-word for the two psalms. It not only means "thanks" but also "praise", a *confession* of praise and again a *confession* of sin. It is the same word.

Reflection over the great prayers of acknowledgement and confession which we find in Scripture, such as those in Ezra and Nehemiah and then the one in the third chapter of Daniel, will show that they are combinations of praise, thanksgiving and admission:

> O my God, I am ashamed and blush to lift my face to thee, my God... From the days of our fathers to this day we have been in great guilt; but in our captivity thou hast not abandoned us. Thou hast saved us, shown us favour, freed a remnant of us; brightened our eyes and granted us a little consolation in our bondage (see Ezra 9:6ff).

Confession and praise alternate: the background is that of the "*confessio laudis*" and the "*confessio vitae*" [cf. Peter's "confession" or testimony – Matthew 16:16], not self-torture and resentment.

For the rest, those who are acquainted with the *Confessions* of St Augustine know how this great saint could marvellously combine in his book the confession of praise with the confession of his own sins.

Let us read another example from the prayer of Nehemiah:

> Stand up and bless the Lord your God from everlasting to everlasting! Blessed be his glorious name which is exalted above all blessing and praise... Thou art the Lord, thou alone. But we have acted with pride: our fathers stiffened their neck and they refused to obey. But thou art a God ready to forgive, gracious and merciful... Thou gavest thy good Spirit. Nevertheless they were disobedient and rebelled against thee. In the time of their suffering they cried to thee and thou didst hear them (See Nehemiah 9).

This long prayer is a continual interaction of praise, thanksgiving, confession and recognition of blame. In it are to be found the truth of ourselves, humility and the joy of recognizing our lowliness before so great and good a God.

It would also be an advantage to stop and consider in the same way the third chapter of the Book of Daniel where the prayer of Azariah is given:

> Blessed art thou, O Lord, God of our fathers. For thou art just in all that thou hast done. We have sinfully and lawlessly departed from thee, and have not obeyed thy commandments. Yet with a contrite heart and a humble spirit may we be accepted.

That prayer is like our Psalm 50 [51], taking up some of its expressions, expanding the sense of praise and the confession of sin. To confess oneself in praise was so habitual to the Hebrew that even the Pharisee in the Gospel parable starts his confession with praise: "God, I thank thee that I am not like other men" (Luke 18:9-14).

The Pharisee's mistake when beginning with the *toda* lies in combining the *confessio laudis* and the *confessio vitae* without first laying his poverty before the mercy and goodness of God, that poverty which on the other hand the publican recognizes, simply and courageously: "God, be merciful to me a sinner". That is to say: You are great, compassionate, powerful, and I am poor. You will save me and I will praise you for your great power.

You see then the background, the tone, the form that our confession ought to have: a background of *toda*.

The importance of forgiveness

To clarify the many difficulties concerning the subject of God's forgiveness and God's saving judgement, I have found it very useful to distinguish three moments in the New Testament.

In New Testament language these would be called *kairoi:* three hours or times in salvation history, distinct from one another, when God exercises judgement on sinful humanity.

(a)   The first moment is baptismal forgiveness. It is the forgiveness or allowance made for a person who is taking the first step to enter into the Covenant by asking for baptism.

It is God's first great pardon, which can better be called a free pardon. God decides gratuitously to confer grace and mercy. He makes no conditions, not even one of good conduct, because all have sinned and all need his mercy.

All he asks is faith in his Son, Messiah and Saviour. If you believe in Jesus Christ, be baptized and you will be saved (see Mark 16:16).

The sinner is one who is pardoned, and with that fundamental forgiveness he is created anew, and accepted into the Covenant. It is a judgement of the Most High which is complete pardon in respect of the sinful human condition.

(b)   A second moment is the remission of sins or the saving judgement given by absolution within the dialogue of Confession.

If a person who has entered into the Covenant with God, fails to keep its precepts and offends against God, Christ and the Church, forgiveness is offered in Confession. In the case of baptism no confession of sins or absolution takes place, but for one who has already entered the Covenant, the saving judgement requires confession of sins.

The Word of God rebukes the person who acknowledges a specific offence, who admits to being a sinner and who asks to be made new by the power of the Spirit ("Create in me a clean heart, O Lord"). God then creates the heart of that person anew.

It is thus a confession of sin and an act of forgiveness in a dialogue between the individual and God, taking place within the Church that community which has been wounded by the breaking of the Covenant.

(c) The third moment is that of the Last Judgement. Here the New Testament is quite specific, and we ought not to ignore it.

At the end of an historical period, at the end of an individual life, at the end of history, the Messiah will come as judge of the living and the dead, to give each one according to what he or she has done. In the final judgement no more allowance is made, nor will there be any time for dialogue. It is judgement according to the truth.

The seriousness of the sacramental confession of sins lies in taking up a correct position between the general baptismal pardon, by which we are saved through simple adhesion in faith to Christ, and the last judgement at which each one comes to be scrupulously weighed according to past actions.

The dialogue, the forgiveness given in the Sacrament of Penance, stands between these two realities and helps us grow towards that maturity which allows us to present ourselves confidently before the final judgement of God.

There is therefore great importance in this penitential dialogue. In it is revealed God's goodness which, through the Church, gradually restores us to our dignity and prepares us for a divine judgement which will unveil the wonders of God's love working in each one of us, poor sinners.

Personal questions

I suggest four questions for you to think over.

− Do I let myself be challenged by the Word of God? Do I think of the Word not only as instruction or consolation but also as interrogation and admonition, becoming the starting point for the penitential dialogue?

− Do I experience Confession as a real dialogue with the Church against the background of the Covenant? Or do I find it a hurried monologue in which I simply make a tortuous self-examination which leaves me cold and bitter?

− Do I know how to combine *confessio vitae* and

117

confessio laudis? So I prepare for confession and then in confession itself I say: I want to thank God for his goodness to me. Then I go on to consider whether what I have not done for God has more weight than what I have done against him.

– Do I know how to correct others? This question may perhaps surprise you. In reality it follows as a social consequence from what we have been saying, in the context of home, work and community.

Do I realize that the Word of God is not only a stimulus or a consolation but also a firm and loving reproach? And there is nothing more difficult than to reproach firmly and lovingly!

For this reason many people prefer to let things pass. They would rather criticize people behind their back, or prefer an empty, general complaint. There are few who are strong enough to administer a reproof modelled on the Word of God, that is, one which is true, just, capable of imparting a shock and at the same time full of love. Such a reproof has the ability to initiate a dialogue in hope, an admission and acceptance of what has to be done, so that a person may be restored to the truth. Otherwise we might be content to denigrate or criticize because we do not really seek the good of others.

In New Testament times the practice of fraternal correction was very common, a practice which then spread throughout the Church although today badly neglected. "If you have anything against your brother, go and tell him his fault between him and you alone and you will have gained your brother" (Matthew 18:15).

How many are the times when we don't do that! How often we don't confront our brother in love to help him.

We are afraid to love as God loves.

Let us pray now for one another saying:

Lord, open our eyes to know the riches of your Word and to express it as it pleases you. Let us find again the joy of your presence.

Lord, help us to make a sacramental confession which will bring us back to you in truth, and will give us the strength to share in your word which loves, corrects and saves.

6
Sacramental penance

A reading from the Holy Gospel according to Luke
(19:1-10):

> He entered Jericho and was passing through. And there
> was a man named Zacchaeus; he was a chief tax collector,
> and rich. And he sought to see who Jesus was, but could
> not, on account of the crowd, because he was small of
> stature. So he ran on ahead and climbed up into a sycamore
> tree to see him, for he was to pass that way. And when
> Jesus came to the place, he looked up and said to him,
> "Zacchaeus, make haste and come down; for I must stay
> at your house today." So he made haste and came down,
> and received him joyfully. And when they saw it they all
> murmured, "He has gone in to be the guest of a man who
> is a sinner." And Zacchaeus stood and said to the Lord,
> "Behold, Lord, the half of my goods I give to the poor;
> and if I have defrauded any one of anything, I restore it
> fourfold." And Jesus said to him, "Today salvation has
> come to this house, since he also is a son of Abraham. For
> the Son of man came to seek and to save the lost."

Then wilt thou delight in right sacrifices,
    in burnt offerings and whole burnt offerings.

Now let us seek the Lord while meditating on some of the
final words in Psalm 50 [51].

Exegetes in fact question whether these closing lines,
beginning at verse 17, belong to the psalm or not. Some
think it is a liturgical appendage, national in character, added

121

at this point to turn the song from being the supplication of an individual into a collective song.

It speaks of Sion, Jerusalem, its walls and its sacrifices: all of which is concerned with the Temple worship and the very life of the city, whereas in the preceding lines it is a person seeking reconciliation with God.

Political overtones of the psalm

So we find ourselves in a landscape where the course of the individual journey is merged in the liturgical life of the whole community of Israel as well as the whole city.

We could say that we are invited to meditate upon the social and political overtones of the psalm of penitence and the way of reconciliation which it proposes. Some words with which we began come in again here. Referring to the Synod of Bishops I stressed that one of the agreed points at the synodal assembly was the conviction that there is no social, civic or political reconciliation without a change of heart, and that there is no change of heart without repercussions in society in general.

It is on this basis that I want to deepen our understanding of that point in the Sacrament of Reconciliation actually called "penance" or "satisfaction". It is a question then of those acts, prayers and undertakings which the priest confessor asks us to perform as sign and fruit of our conversion.

The penance

When I, as minister of the sacrament, consider the "penance", I begin to feel a little uneasy. For a priest it is perhaps one of the most difficult moments.

The priest asks himself: What penance is really appropriate to the path this penitent is following? How can I in such a short space of time single out the penance which will be the fruit of a specific conversion for this person? What would be really useful for expressing this particular life's journey?

You see, the confessor often escapes from this difficulty by suggesting one or other of the set prayers. These are very good and important, but nevertheless they do not always seem suitable for the path this person is following.

This is the real trouble about the actual penitential part of the Sacrament, when one would like to get away from routine, habit, formality, and adapt to the needs of the person.

On the other hand I am convinced – as we all are – that it is one of those occasions when the Church is closest, in concrete form, to the one fulfilling the penitential journey. It is true the Church is near at every stage of the Sacrament: in the examination of conscience, helping out with questions; at the time of "sorrow for sin", offering the example of the saints in making a resolution; above all being transparent to Christ and his mercy when accepting and absolving in the name of the Lord.

When suggesting the "penance" though, the Church wants to adapt very specially to each person, in his or her unique individuality.

One ought then to be a master in the ways of penance for the penitent to show, according to the word of John the Baptist, "fruit that benefits repentance", a sign of a heart desiring to be renewed.

Zacchaeus

Bearing in mind then the difficulty the "penance" poses for the priest who is administering the Sacrament, I invite you to meditate on the passage in the Gospel which speaks about Zacchaeus (Luke 19:1-10).

We can call it a passage that shows a penitential encounter between this man and Jesus. It is a singularly historic story because it expresses a permanent reality.

In this meeting, Zacchaeus carries out a series of successive exterior and interior acts, some of which are the prelude, others the consequence, of Christ's word of forgiveness.

The interior act which Zacchaeus accomplishes is his desire to see Jesus. It is an intensely strong desire which we might almost call "ecstatic", one which takes Zacchaeus out of himself. Indeed it is not likely to be mere curiosity which made him run to see Jesus. He is moved by a profound desire from within and already it is a half-formed love for Jesus which prompts him to an external action.

The external action which Zacchaeus does is to climb up a tree. It is surprising that a man like him, an official, starts running along the road and then goes up a tree, something he would not have done in normal cirumstances. He is a person who is undergoing an attack of love so strong as to make him forget his usual habits, his reputation, his dignity and his vanity.

We see how the friendly word of Jesus drops into this intense love of Zacchaeus. "I must stay at your house today." It is a lovely saying: I am coming home with you today and I want you to invite me to dinner.

This expression of familiarity surprises Zacchaeus and evokes acts which are no longer signs of promise but of conversion:

(a) the outward action is that Zacchaeus welcomes Jesus joyfully;

(b) the inward action is that Zacchaeus decides to give to the poor half of what he has, and to make reparation in an extraordinary measure for the wrong done.

Zacchaeus says: "Lord I now give the half of my goods to the poor and if I have defrauded anyone I restore it fourfold." It is the penitent, social, civic and community effect of the way he has been following. It is the "fruit of repentance" flowing from his reconciliation.

Joy and resolution

However, there are still two things to underline in this journey of Zacchaeus.

First of all the joy with which he accompanies his action, a joy which makes him extraordinarily – we might almost say recklessly – generous is beyond all calculation. It could be pointed out that if he gives half his goods to the poor the other half won't be enough to restore the fourfold! Zacchaeus has lost his sense of proportion. He has been transformed by friendship and reconciliation with Jesus and so what is important to him is to let the abounding joy of it ring round him, as a sign of his conversion.

The first fruit then of the penitential encounter is joy, welling up in us, which makes us do with ease things that we would not have been prepared to do before hearing the word of Jesus.

The second point to underline in Zacchaeus' journey is that he himself suggests to Jesus the "penance" he wants to do and Jesus approves it. Zacchaeus suggests something uncharacteristic of a greedy, scheming, covetous person like himself.

He knew how to pick on his weak points and to base his renewal on this. For him the "fruit of repentance" is generosity to the poor, prompt reparation for the wrong he has done to others (not long prayer formulas, not pilgrimages, not external acts which are not suitable in this case). It is his own personal and exactly right for him. Jesus gives his approval and says: "Today salvation has come to this house."

Now we may return to our initial question. What can I, as the priest administering the Sacrament of Reconciliation, give as a penance suitable to the penitent before me? How can I help this person to bear fruit worthy of repentance?

The answer suggested by the Gospel passage is very simple. Perhaps it is the penitent who can help the confessor. Perhaps it is the one who has started a penitential dialogue with me who can suggest what will help in bringing forth fruit worthy of repentance. Instead of asking myself, as the priest, "What should I give for a penance?" I can ask this sister or brother who has come to me: "What penance do you think would be useful to you? What good work or prayer or reparation corresponds to this point on your journey?"

Each one, therefore, is in a position to help the confessor in establishing what penance would be an expression of a genuine penitential journey.

Instead of lamenting that the penance is unsuitable, and only an external formality that is always the same, we can, in a broader dialogue, suggest what we consider an important sign of the conversion we have requested from God, as a fruit of the Holy Spirit. We call him to us with the words of the psalm: "Create in me a clean heart, O God, and put a new and right spirit within me... take not thy holy Spirit from me. Restore to me the joy of thy salvation..."

Personal questions

I would now like to propose two questions for you to reflect on quietly.

– Does the joy of Zacchaeus go with me in the Sacrament of Reconciliation? If it is not ordinarily with me, why not? I am speaking of a deep-seated joy, not something superficial. This is a joy which may not be strongly felt emotionally but which ought to be there deep down and move the soul to generosity.

If this fundamental joy is not there, the reason might perhaps be sought in some error in following the procedures for reconciliation about which we said something at the beginning. We may have a wrong idea of God, of his mercy and of his loving initiatives; or we may not trust enough in the Church on our journey; or our sorrow which does not spring from a genuine dialogue with Christ and an inner contemplation with the Father.

There are various reasons which each one can think of to understand why joy does not ordinarily accompany the Sacrament of Reconciliation.

– The second question calls for a longer silent reflection. If I had to suggest to the priest a penance suitable for me at this point in my life, what would I say?

This is a demanding question because it brings home to us not only failings and sins but also negative tendencies and the need to sort out what can strike at the root of what is wrong in me. We are looking for acts of penance which are a fruit worthy of personal conversion.

If I am aware, for example, that my sins and failings spring from selfishness, there will come to mind as a fitting penance an act of real generosity which will actually cost me a lot. If I find that some of my sins come from sloth, a penance will emerge that is a victory over laziness, greediness, lack of energy, and everything which makes my life idle, listless and boring. If I agree that my failings derive from antipathy, not accepting a particular person, then there will surface a gesture of attentiveness for that person, something simple but which really involves me.

Let us pray to the Lord:

Lord, we want to offer you fruit worthy of repentance not only for ourselves but for the whole Church and for all humanity, because we feel in part responsible for each one's journey to conversion.

O Lord, open our hearts, our tongues, our hands so that we may recognize the sign of a new direction, a decided step forward towards you. Do not allow us to fall into routine, laziness and monotony. Give us a holy disquiet so that following our journey towards you we may discover in ourselves again the springs of joy. We ask this for ourselves and for every man and woman around us in our life and work.

7

Witnessing to mercy

A reading from the Holy Gospel according to John (4:1-39):

Now when the Lord knew that the Pharisees had heard that Jesus was making and baptizing more disciples than John (although Jesus himself did not baptize, but only his disciples), he left Judaea and departed again to Galilee. He had to pass through Samaria. So he came to a city of Samaria, called Sychar, near the field that Jacob gave to his son Joseph. Jacob's well was there, and so Jesus, wearied as he was with his journey, sat down beside the well. It was about the sixth hour.

There came a woman of Samaria to draw water. Jesus said to her, "Give me a drink." For his disciples had gone away into the city to buy food. The Samaritan woman said to him, "How is it that you, a Jew, ask a drink of me, a woman of Samaria?" For Jews have no dealings with Samaritans. Jesus answered her, "If you knew the gift of God, and who it is that is saying to you, 'Give me a drink,' you would have asked him, and he would have given you living water." The woman said to him, "Sir, you have nothing to draw with, and the well is deep; where do you get that living water? Are you greater than our father Jacob, who gave us the well, and drank from it himself, and his sons, and his cattle?" Jesus said to her, "Everyone who drinks of this water will thirst again, but whoever drinks of the water that I shall give him will never thirst; the water that I shall give him will become in him a spring of water welling up to eternal life." The woman said to him, "Sir, give me this water, that I may not thirst, nor come here to draw."

Jesus said to her, "Go, call your husband, and come here." The woman answered him, "I have no husband." Jesus said to her, "You are right in saying, 'I have no husband'; for you have had five husbands, and he whom you now have is not your husband; this you said truly." The woman said to him, "Sir, I perceive that you are a prophet. Our fathers worshipped on this mountain; and you say that in Jerusalem is the place where men ought to worship." Jesus said to her, "Woman, believe me, the hour is coming when neither on this mountain nor in Jerusalem will you worship the Father. You worship what you do not know; we worship what we know, for salvation is from the Jews. But the hour is coming, and now is, when the true worshippers will worship the Father in spirit and truth, for such the Father seeks to worship him. God is spirit, and those who worship him must worship in spirit and truth." The woman said to him, "I know that Messiah is coming (he who is called Christ); when he comes, he will show us all things." Jesus said to her, "I who speak to you am he."

Just then his disciples came. They marvelled that he was talking with a woman, but none said, "What do you wish?" or, "Why are you talking with her?" So the woman left her water jar, and went away into the city, and said to the people, "Come, see a man who told me all that I ever did. Can this be the Christ?" They went out of the city and were coming to him.

Meanwhile the disciples besought him, saying, "Rabbi, eat." But he said to them, "I have food to eat of which you do not know." So the disciples said to one another, "Has anyone brought him food?" Jesus said to them, "My food is to do the will of him who sent me, and to accomplish his work. Do you not say, 'There are yet four months, then comes the harvest'? I tell you, lift up your eyes, and see how the fields are already white for harvest. He who reaps receives wages, and gathers fruit for eternal life, so that sower and reaper may rejoice together. For here the saying holds true, 'One sows and another reaps.' I sent you to reap that for which you did not labour; others have laboured, and you have entered into their labour."

Many Samaritans from that city believed in him because of the woman's testimony, "He told me all that I ever did."

Then I will teach transgressors thy ways,
    and sinners will return to thee.

O Lord, open thou my lips,
    and my mouth shall show forth thy praise.

I would like to reflect now on the necessity of being witnesses to God's mercy.

Here I take my inspiration from the end of Psalm 50 [51] where precisely this theme of being sent on a mission is expressed: "I will teach transgressors thy ways... my tongue will sing aloud of thy deliverance... open thou my lips and my mouth shall show forth thy praise." The one who has travelled the way to penitence senses this mission as the final point of what has been done and undergone.

The psalmist's experience

We note first of all that the psalmist expresses his missionary task in a precise fashion, corresponding with the way he has come: I will make those with no road understand that there is a road, and along it you, Lord, are coming to meet them. I will make them understand not as though I was giving a lecture or an admonition but as a witness to what has happened to me.

You see the force of this testimony. He has followed a truly penitential road and can help others to see that there is a way out. It is not merely a general exit or one where you have to play the stoic or the hero but a way forward, along which God himself comes to meet you, in Jesus, as he came to me.

More than once in a lifetime it happens that it is just the one who has emerged from some dark tunnel who is singularly fitted to say to others: Courage, there is surely a way out for you too!

This is expressed by the psalmist freely and outspokenly as though he were uttering words he has been given for that purpose. The three things which express human speech – tongue, lips, mouth – are being turned here to a missionary use. Tongue, lips, mouth open not because coerced, not out of duty, but in an outpouring of the fullness within.

We know very well that a message given with the mouth half shut is not of much use, and at times even counter-productive. On the contrary, a testimony springing from an exultant tongue, a mouth that must open, lips moving joyously, is truly to be respected and worth listening to.

We could at once ask ourselves: What of my testimony? Does it come from a half-open mouth, lips searching hesitantly and laboriously for the right words? In that case it is not the result of an experience but rather of something not yet born in me.

Or is it a testimony which is spontaneous, free, joyous, in which the words come out freely? In that case, you are working in me, Lord, with your grace. It is your Spirit which opens my mouth so that I can sing your praise in love, so that I can teach others that there is a way when they think there is nothing that can be done. Lord, open my mouth, especially in difficult situations in which I might stay tongue-tied, not knowing what to say, and when it really might seem to me there was absolutely no hope.

The Samaritan woman's experience

St John's Gospel, chapter 4, gives us another example of a mouth open to give testimony, convinced and convincing: the Samaritan woman.

It is a passage which can provide a comment on what we have been saying in this chapter, because this also shows a journey of penance and a point when a person encounters the truth of herself before Christ, and the truth of Christ as saviour and friend.

At the end of the journey, we find the opening of heart and mouth: "So the woman left her water jar and went away to the city and said to the people: 'Come and see a man who told me all that I ever did. Can this be the Christ?'"

Notice the fine detail: "she left her water jar". This woman had come to fetch water. That pitcher was precious to her, her daily life was bound up with it. But just now all that is forgotten, and the brimming pitcher left lying at the edge of the well is the sign of an existence the woman has henceforth abandoned, the sign that an obsessive urge has fallen away from her. Like the two disciples at Emmaus, who left their meal half finished and ran to Jerusalem, the Samaritan woman runs back up the road and into the town and goes around telling what has happened to her. True, she announces it awkwardly enough: "The Christ, maybe?" She is not a very effective herald, at least from the theological point of view. And yet these words are a most efficacious witness because they derive from a lived experience. The people have before them a person who is not speaking with carefully prepared words, is not repeating a lesson, but speaking in broken sentences almost, yet from the heart and moved like someone who has had a striking experience which she must communicate.

The Samaritan woman's lips are opened, and her tongue loosened. In an explosion of joy she speaks simply and truthfully of God's mercy to her.

Proclaiming God's mercy

In view of the psalmist's experience and that of the Samaritan woman, we ought to ask ourselves what our missionary testimony of mercy should be. We are in fact called upon to witness to the grace which has drawn us and welcomed us along our journey of penance.

In the encyclical *Dives in Misericordia*, Pope John Paul II expresses this task in two places.

In the first place he speaks of the general duty to bear witness:

> The Church of our time must become more particularly and profoundly conscious of the need to bear witness in her whole mission to God's mercy, following in the footsteps of the tradition of the Old and the New Covenant, and above all of Jesus Christ himself and his Apostles (VII 13-15).

Witness to mercy is then a duty for our time. The Pope seems almost to have the impression that the Church needs to be exhorted, today above all, to ponder on the necessity of bearing witness to God's mercy.

At a later point he underlines three ways in which witness is to be given.

> Professing it in the first place as a salvific truth of faith necessary in a life consistent with faith; then seeking to introduce it into life and incarnate it for the faithful, as far as possible, for all people of good will. Finally, the Church has the right and the duty to appeal to God's mercy, imploring his mercy in prayer. (*ibid.*)

It is easy to understand how we can give testimony to God's mercy by professing it. Each time we approach the Sacrament of Reconciliation we also make a *confessio fidei*, that is, we proclaim that God is Lord of our life and greater than our sin; that his mercy triumphs over the weakness of our human existence and the misery of humanity's sin. Thus we confess and proclaim the mercy of God.

Incarnating mercy

The second way of witnessing to divine mercy suggested by the Pope is more difficult. It is no small matter to incarnate the mercy of God in our life. Rather, it is so difficult that

134

at times it leaves us perplexed and afraid. It leaves us speechless and unable to go further along the path of mission and witness. On the other hand, if we do not succeed in giving testimony to God's mercy, the credibility of the Church and our Christian life is brought into question.

I would like to help you grasp this difficulty by reflecting on three situations in which we could find ourselves.

(a) Ordinary situations. What does it mean to incarnate mercy or witness mercy? Concretely it means putting into practice that plea we make in the Our Father: "Forgive us our trespasses as we forgive those who trespass against us." It means knowing how to forgive seventy times seven.

That is difficult to start with for all sorts of reasons as we know well enough. It is so difficult that we often push aside this precept of forgiveness and so it remains irrelevant to our lives. Yet it is a necessary daily witness to mercy enjoined by God: "If you do not forgive those who do wrong to you, neither will your Father forgive you" (see Matthew 6:15).

(b) More complex situations. There are cases in which mutual exchange comes into play. Sometimes it is not enough to forgive, as though we had only to do a favour to someone, but we have to beg for forgiveness ourselves. We need to recognize that we have been offended but that we have given cause for it. We have been the object of some injustice, but have also behaved in a manner not entirely just. All this is very difficult.

There is another rather difficult case for give and take in daily life which is an absolute necessity because it forms the warp and woof of life. We have already met this above. It is not enough to forgive. We need to know how to guide another and we need to know how to correct another. Fraternal correction, so important for the Christian community and a practice of the early Church, requires much love and much humility. Yet we often cut it out of our sphere of action because it appears too risky, or even impossible or ineffective, and in this way we do not testify enough to God's mercy.

Let us ask ourselves in all sincerity: How do I deal with

135

these opportunities to witness, not only in words, but also in deed, to the mercy of the One who has loved us, welcomed us and refashioned us from within, the One who has faith in us?

(c)There are, finally, cases which are conflicting, where mercy apparently demands a certain way of acting whereas justice requires another.

These are extremely difficult situations and we do not always succeed in finding a satisfactory solution: situations which cause great suffering in the Church, in society or in the family. In trying to practise mercy we end up absolutely fearing to do wrong to others. That creates an apparent conflict of values and we no longer know what to choose or we choose something which is unsatisfactory.

People who have to cope with responsibility find that many such cases make them suffer to the extent that they are unable to see how unjust they might be in their exercise of mercy. This suffering they should offer to God because it is the only thing they can do.

Then there are cases in which performing an act of mercy involves the loss of that minimum of self-possession which is necessary if I am to give myself, and so I do not do it. How often generous people reach their limit and realize they can go no further. There are built-in limits to our human weakness which is extremely painful. To go beyond a certain limit is equivalent to losing possession of oneself and things turn out differently from what we intend. This measure of necessary prudence makes us realize how difficult it is to give a really outstanding witness to mercy. All that remains to us then is to suffer and pray, for ourselves and for others.

Imploring mercy

The Pope, in *Dives in Misericordia*, after having spoken about trying to introduce an incarnate mercy into life, adds that there is need to "implore God's mercy in the face of all the manifestations of physical and moral evil, before all the threats that cloud the whole horizon of the life of humanity today."

We ought to be assured that this entreaty is an active, genuine resistance to evil, and profoundly displeasing to the Enemy.

I was greatly struck by a passage from Simone Weil where she writes:

> It is not so hard to renounce something pleasant however intoxicating or to submit to pain however violent. We see this daily in ordinary people. But it is infinitely difficult to renounce even a very slight pleasure or espouse an extremely small suffering *for God alone*; for the true God, for the one who is in heaven and not elsewhere. Because, when we do this, it is not taking on suffering but death. A more radical death than the physical, a death which our very nature holds in horror.

On the contrary, that is the right moment for conquering evil: for believing in the value of a supplication which does not have immediately obvious results.

Our prayer of petition, above all when it appears that there is nothing else to be done, is a true way of resisting evil. We must not then be afraid of dryness and abandon prayer as we are often tempted to do because we do not immediately succeed in crushing the evil. It is through that enduring supplication, agonizing sometimes even to tears, that God will enable us to show mercy and love even in such circumstances.

Conclusion

This is therefore the real meaning of being witnesses to divine mercy: 'I will teach your ways to the erring.' Recognizing that we are all very far from this serious witness to mercy, we should return to the creation prayer of Psalm 50 [51]:

"Create in me a clean heart, O God" because I haven't one and you will have to create it in me as a new thing.

"Put a new and right spirit within me" at times when my spirit fails in weariness and fear.

"Restore to me the joy of thy salvation, and uphold me with a willing spirit" to be a testimony of your mercy before so many brothers and sisters who are looking for this witness to you, merciful Father, you who have loved me and called me, who have brought me with many others along the journey to conversion and mercy.

I would like to conclude with the words of Charles de Foucauld. After pointing to the *Miserere* as a prayer which mirrors our experience, a daily prayer to raise us up to God, he says:

[This prayer] starts from a consideration of ourselves and the consciousness of our sins and rises finally to the contemplation of God, through love of our neighbour and the desire for the conversion of all.

So it is a universal prayer from which none is excluded. It shows the reality of our human history as an involvement and a mutual presence in each other's lives. In this prayer, we remember, forgive, support each other on the hard road of Gospel conversion, an authentic return to Christ.

By praying Psalm 50 [51] we relive this weary way and with that the immense joy in the Spirit which is poured out on our life and we grow towards the mysterious presence of God, of Christ, in human history.

I ask the Lord that through the memory of this psalm in our hearts we may keep also the memory of those wonderful moments when we have experienced friendship, faith and humility on asking forgiveness. And finally I beseech the Lord that he may light our way with the splendour of his countenance and sustain us with the grace of his Spirit.

Also by Cardinal Carlo-Maria Martini:

THE WOMAN
AMONG HER PEOPLE
A spiritual journey
into the "planet woman"

Biblical meditations given by Cardinal Carlo-Maria Martini to the women religious of his archdiocese.

In these meditations the Cardinal looks through the lens of Gospel passages at some women portrayed therein and then observes them in the light of Mary. These meditations – a simple and profound compendium of theology – are beneficial to every Christian in search of the God of Revelation.

In an original and impressive way, the Cardinal, one of the most authoritative figures in the Church today, brings faith down to the level of concrete daily life.

ISBN 085439 297 1

MINISTERS OF THE GOSPEL

The Second Vatican Council has made us all aware of the
priesthood of the laity. This means that every Christian is a
minister of the Gospel – an evangelizer; we are called to witness to Christ's redeeming love.

How do we do this? Cardinal Martini suggests new ways of
implementing the Gospel message, but he speaks less of
doing than of being – being open to God's Word of saving
love, being a channel of that love to a searching and often be-
wildered world. These meditations on St Luke's Gospel
show us how an evangelizer is formed in the school of
Christ.

ISBN 085439 220 3

DAVID
sinner and believer

A collection of fourteen meditations and seven homilies.
Adopting the Ignatian method, Cardinal Martini reflects
on the figure of King David, with the aim of deepening the
reader's awareness of God's saving plan which ultimately
became manifest in Christ. The Old and New Testament
are in this way read in parallel, according to the *lectio
divina* method: reading of the text; meditation and prayer
based on the Word; contemplation of biblical characters
or scenes.

The book offers genuine and profoundspiritual
nourishment to those who wish to be initiated into the art
of reading the Bible; it is an authoritiative and easy guide.

ISBN 085439 322 6

IN THE THICK OF
HIS MINISTRY

Cardinal Martini, reflecting on some passages of the Second Letter to the Corinthians, delves deeply into Paul. Here "we find Paul in the thick of his ministry. After twenty years of it, during which he passed through so many trials, disappointments and difficulties, he speaks as a servant of the Gospel in the midst of the daily grind. So we feel he is very close to us". The Cardinal draws up a good picture of the pastor serving the Gospel in the Christian community and helping it grow in the faith. We are shown the richness and possibilities of this life "even though some days may be beset with sufferings and misunderstandings." Though initially intended for young priests, the book is of interest to anyone committed to the service of the Gospel.

ISBN 085439 336 6

THE TESTIMONY OF
ST PAUL

The Apostle Paul has reached the last hour of his life and faces martyrdom for the One whom he has served and proclaimed far and wide. If we had met him on the road and asked him what events in his life had been the most significant, what would have he answered?
What would have been his final testimony? Cardinal Martini sets out to answer these questions in a series of meditations based on St Paul's life and letters. He seeks to enter into Paul's thoughts and attitudes – and asks us some searching questions about our own.

ISBN 085439 221 1